The Non-Technical Founder

THE NON-TECHNICAL FOUNDER

How a 16-Year Old Built a $100,000 Software Company Without Writing ANY Code

JOSH MACDONALD

NEW YORK

LONDON • NASHVILLE • MELBOURNE • VANCOUVER

The Non-Technical Founder

How a 16-Year Old Built a $100,000 Software Company
Without Writing Any Code

Published in New York, New York, by Morgan James Publishing. Morgan James is a trademark of Morgan James, LLC. www.MorganJamesPublishing.com

The Morgan James Speakers Group can bring authors to your live event. For more information or to book an event visit The Morgan James Speakers Group at www.TheMorganJamesSpeakersGroup.com.

ISBN 9781683507598 paperback
ISBN 9781683507604 eBook
Library of Congress Control Number: 2017913995

Cover Design by:
Rachel Lopez
www.r2cdesign.com

Interior Design by:
Chris Treccani
www.3dogcreative.net

In an effort to support local communities, raise awareness and funds, Morgan James Publishing donates a percentage of all book sales for the life of each book to Habitat for Humanity Peninsula and Greater Williamsburg.

Get involved today! Visit
www.MorganJamesBuilds.com

Dedicated to my late grandfather, John Johnson.

TABLE OF CONTENTS

• • • • • • • •

CONTRIBUTORS

• • • • • • • •

This book, and the value it contains, would not be possible without the help of my amazing contributors. Their contributions are included throughout the book in their respective areas of specialization. Each contributor is friendly, intelligent, and approachable. If you have any questions on what they say, you can reach out to them on Twitter, or check out their published works.

WHO IS THIS BOOK FOR?

• • • • • • •

It's 5:15 AM on a chilly fall morning. Don reaches out from under the covers and grabs his phone. He shields his eyes from the bright light, then begins flicking through the dozens of notifications that have curiously appeared overnight. They're all from a 15-year-old kid he had talked to briefly on a business forum a few weeks ago.

Don starts to take count of the texts. Throughout the entire night, a new text was sent every 15 minutes. Each contained a different outlandish and unfocused business idea. Don is a successful businessman with real experience, so he could have answered each and every text with certainty, but this was absurd! It seemed the kid had no respect for Don or his time.

Remembering his own beginnings, Don smiles. The kid has potential. But he's going to need to someday get focused some day if he hopes to see success.

The kid from the business forum is me, and Don is one of my mentors. I did eventually find my focus. I thought of an idea, held my mind to it, hired a developer to turn my idea into reality… then sold over $100,000 of my new software in the year after launch.

This book is for everyone who wants to succeed as a software entrepreneur who may not have yet found a mentor like Don. As for me, I am not well-known. I grew up in a rural town with shoddy internet connection. I worked on my entrepreneurial projects after school. I didn't attend Harvard, but rather the best local option I could afford. With all that in mind, I still found success selling software I created. If you can relate to my beginnings at all, then this book was written for you.

You are about to read a practical guide on bootstrapping your own software idea. When it comes to learning, first-hand experience is always best. I've been in the internet business industry since 2009. That's a lot of first-hand experience! I have included all of it in the pages beyond, as well as guidelines as to how you can follow in my footsteps and find success yourself.

Truthfully, these pages could be converted into a 1000-page manual, but the specifics of this industry change too often. Instead, consider this book as a fast-paced learning instrument for you, the reader, to familiarize yourself with the numerous concepts you will need to know in order to get started. As with any project with grand ambitions, you may need to dig further into any concept that interests you in order to find out the recent specifics to understand the concept in full.

WHO AM I, AND HOW DID I END UP
IN THE SOFTWARE INDUSTRY?

· · · · · · · ·

My name is Josh MacDonald. I grew up in what most call "small-town Canada." At the time of writing, I am 21-years-old. I started messing around with internet marketing when I was 14, just a freshman in high school. My first project was an online discussion forum. With a few clicks to install a script and a little bit of troubleshooting, my online discussion forum was up and running. The topic was gaming. Like many kids of that age, I was interested in gaming, and the discussion board had various gaming pages where users could talk to each other. The project didn't last long. I learned my first lesson very quickly. I had seen someone say "if you build it, they will come" somewhere on the internet, and that had stuck with me. But no one came. Lesson #1: A website won't get traffic just because you make it. There are a million other websites exactly like yours. No one cares. You need to promote.

My first thought was advertising. But at that young age, I didn't have a debit or credit card to promote my website with. So I started creating content for YouTube, as that was something I could understand and actually do. I would talk about a gaming tutorial, or a free piece of software, and send YouTube users over to my website if they wanted to get it for themselves. Soon I had hundreds of daily unique visitors. But another problem had popped up. Visitors would read my forum, get what they needed, and leave. I wanted them to stay. So I added a rule to my forum that required users to register and make five posts before they were able to access certain sections. I was encountering problems and learning to solve them on a daily basis.

Before long I had 1,000 registered members. I was floored! I placed Google ads on my website hoping to make money on clicks. I managed to make a few dollars, which was exhilarating. Finally, I had the proof I could show my friends so they would understand that making money online wasn't a scam.

I did earn from that website, but not a whole lot. A few dollars here and there didn't satisfy me. Wanting to make more money, I started offering up my time as a freelance writer. At first, during my early years of high school, I was charging $1 for every 100 words. The gig was great. I got off the bus around 4 PM and went straight to work for my clients. The pay was guaranteed, and it really wasn't hard to clear $30 in a night before I had to stop to tackle my homework (always last minute). After a few weeks of this grind, I finally had enough to try out some new projects that required a little bit of investment.

One of these projects was offering my services as a website builder. At this point, I knew how to build websites and generate ad revenue from them. The process was fairly simple. You see, Google lets you see exactly how much advertisers are paying for an ad click on content related to a particular keyword. I found high-paying keywords that had low competition from other websites in the Google SERPs (search engine result pages). I made websites based around these high-paying keywords, ranked them in Google easily, and cashed in on the free traffic I was getting every time someone clicked on an ad on my website. A single click could easily earn me a few dollars, just like that.

Let me explain how these websites worked. Imagine you have a simple website with a few informational articles on it. That's your "micro niche site." You rank it for the keyword it's built around and receive 100 visitors every day from Google. Your click-through rate (CTR) is 5%, meaning you get five ad clicks per day. If each ad click earns you $2, you make $10 per day of pure profit from your single micro niche site, with no time investment whatsoever.

The potential was enormous. I began to see that these "micro niche sites" were hot items. Many people hadn't figured out what I told you—even adults with real money to invest—and they were eager to get a piece of the micro niche gold rush. (If you had enough of these websites, you would be earning more than you ever could at a job.)

My sites were very basic and had just five articles of 500 words each. I was able to drive sales through various internet marketing forums, in the "Buy/Sell/Trade" section of each forum. To post an ad for your service in one of these sections on one of these forums, you need to pay a $20 to $40 fee. At this point, my freelance writing money came in handy. I overcame the small investment hurdle and I was able to offer my services to thousands of red-hot, hungry buyers. My websites sold fast.

The interesting part of this project is that my service left out the most important part: ranking the website in Google for the desired keyword. I just sold the website, which boasted easy rankability and sky-high ad CTRs, and then let the buyer figure out how to rank the website on his own. I knew a little bit about ranking websites, but not enough to confidently add it as part of my service. Besides, that was an unknown variable. By offering just the website, I was able to control costs easily and minimize customer support needs.

I outsourced the time-consuming content creation part of the website building process, which limited my work to finding profitable keywords and putting together the structure of the website. I was working less than I did when I was freelance writing, but earning much more.

These types of opportunities are in abundance. You can set up a small but profitable business and quickly start earning more than you ever would at a job or as a freelancer. My website creation service had enormous value, but truth be told, there were others who offered the exact same thing as I did. Luckily, there was plenty to go around, and I was steadily earning a respectable amount.

What I was doing eventually made its way around school because, as expected, my friends told everyone. You'd be surprised at how a small amount of success can bring about big change. There was this teacher—let's call her Mrs. P., she taught my English class—and from what I could tell, she would mark my work lower than everyone else, even if the quality was similar, or better. One day, to test my theory, I let someone copy my answers, then checked the marks afterwards. Sure enough, I had received lower marks than my classmate, even though the substance of the answers was the exact same. These incidents continued, and escalated when she sent me to the office for having my phone out during attendance, which was generally frowned upon, but nowhere severe enough of an offense to send a student to the office.

Mrs. P. taught me a valuable lesson. There are some people who just get jealous. I wasn't pulling in 6-figures yet. Still, she knew I had an "internet company" that was doing well, and as a teacher with her salary, it's my belief she resented me for it. The good news is that this was a cheap lesson, because to be quite honest with you, I wasn't too concerned with a slightly lower mark in English class. The micro niche website creation service was eating up all of my time, but I wanted to go even bigger to take advantage of this gold rush in a serious way.

Enter Keyword Scout.

THE RISE—AND FALL—OF KEYWORD SCOUT

· · · · · · · ·

I had my micro niche business running smoothly, but finding the keywords was taking up a whole lot of my time. I had learned there were two ways to automating tasks in the online business world. You can train assistants—called VAs (virtual assistants)—to perform the tasks for you. Or, you can build a software that does everything for you automatically.

I thought about hiring VAs, but keyword research is complex, and relies on certain concepts that are difficult to teach. On top of that, most affordable VAs are from third-world countries, and the language barrier added another very frustrating layer of difficulty to this approach.

After looking at products on the market that could perform the research as I needed, I saw that there were indeed some available, but none had all the features I needed. There was room for improvement. So instead of spending money on a license for a subpar program, I did it manually and let my profits stack up, until I reached the point where I could hire a programmer to make a new program for me.

I hired a programmer from India on oDesk, now known as Upwork. Upwork is like Craigslist mixed with Yelp when you are trying to hire someone online. You can search for freelancers who can do what you want, message them, invite them to bid on your project, and more. You can also check their reviews.

I didn't want to have any problems, so before I hired anyone, I vigorously read through their ratings and reviews to make sure I was making a smart choice. Hasn't worked in 6 months? Next. Only completes half of the projects he is hired for? Next. Excellent reviews, but a few mediocre ones? Next.

I eventually found someone who impressed me, and he was able to complete the project to my specifications. Once the software was complete, there was a small hiccup, as the programmer had only sent me the executable file, not the readable source code, which I wanted. When I asked for the source code, he ended up blackmailing me, but after some back-and-forth, and an additional "fee" that was never mentioned, I had everything I needed to proceed.

At the start, I planned to use the software just for my use. It was robust, but I imagined that everyone else was already using one of the big-name tools on the market; many of which had more features. I started showing my software to my industry friends. To my surprise, they saw value in it, and they told me that everyone needed it, and wanted it. My software worked well, but its real value was that it had all of the needs of keyword research under one roof, in a spectacular design. Other software had more features, but mine had the ones people needed. So, I decided to offer it to the public as well.

Now I had to figure out pricing. I decided to set a recurring price of $39.99. Selling it as a service, and not as a once-off sale, proved to be one of the better decisions I have made. Getting customers was easier, and once the customers saw the value in the software, they continued to subscribe every month, which over time earned me far more than a realistic once-off sale ever could have.

Turns out people understand this marketing strategy well, and before long, I had many customers asking me to offer a lifetime, once-off price to access the software. Though the $39.99 price was doing well, I figured I should please my customers, and started selling lifetime licenses in addition to the monthly option.

The lifetime licenses were very popular! I sold them for $197 each. My bank account balance was increasing fast and I was psyched. But in the long run, this decision to sell lifetime licenses turned out to be a bad one. Most of the lifetime customers would have become monthly customers because they needed the tool badly. Monthly customers would have earned me far more over time. And as the months went on, the lifetime customers still expected the same consistency of updates as monthly customers did, and I hadn't thought of this. In time, I was constantly updating the software for all of my customers, but only a portion were paying me monthly fees. If I had to do it again, I would offer yearly licenses for the long-term option instead of lifetime licenses, therefore, giving my dedicated customers a cheaper option and building a bankroll fast, all while guaranteeing steady earnings for myself in the future.

But we're not there yet. At this point, I was selling $197 lifetime licenses like hotcakes via the "Buy/Sell/Trade" section of various forums, and loving it. When sales slowed, I'd do a sales price of $147 to generate more interest and sales, then increase the price right back to $197 a few days later. By December 2011, sales had really begun to pick up, and I decided to expand into other marketplaces.

I put my ads on a forum called Warrior Forum. Back in the day, Warrior Forum was arguably the largest online marketing forum, and the "Buy/Sell/Trade" had even more activity than the forums I was using currently. The deal used to be that you could list a lifetime advertisement for a cheap fee, so long as you offered an exclusive discount to the members of the forum. I dropped my price even further down to $97 for a lifetime license, and paid the now-nominal $40 fee to get my sales thread approved and listed.

Despite the hubbub of activity, it turned out that merely listing your sales thread is not enough to generate real interest on this particular forum. The community is more tightly knit. The marketplace is driven almost entirely by affiliates—usually, respectable members of the forum—who would market your products to their email lists and take a portion of the sales they make for you. (Most people never discovered this fact, and utilized Warrior Forum to only a fraction of its potential.)

So I thought I should start talking to affiliates. I messaged every affiliate on the forum that I could find. I simply told them how great my product was and the rave reviews it was getting, then asked them if they would promote it. This process was pretty easy to do, as it was a genuinely fantastic product, and was getting genuine rave reviews from customers. Most said no, because even at the reduced price of $97, they thought that price point was far too high. Some big affiliates asked me to lower it. The extra sales were tempting. But I eventually decided against lowering the price, as many users of the software, such as marketing agency owners, clearly had the money to afford it.

I tell you this because in the world of affiliate marketing, stats are everything. The average product price on the Warrior Forum was around $19, because in general that's what produced the best conversion rates at the time. My product was $97, a far cry from $19. And I was just some random guy asking them to promote my product to their extremely valuable lists. To most affiliates, it seemed like a bad idea. They would rather stick to a standard $19 product they knew would work.

In the end, my decision to stick with $97 was a good one, because although I only had a few affiliates at first, they gave me the opportunity to showcase the superior profits of promoting my product as an affiliate. $19 products made more sales, but a sale of my product was worth much more. If an affiliate could send 100 clicks to my product and to a $19 product, sending them to mine would earn him much more money.

Slowly, the affiliates started to pile on, and I was making a healthy amount of sales from my affiliates, without any effort from myself. I would get a new affiliate, he would do the hard work promoting my software. When he made a sale, he would get a percentage of the profit, and I would keep the rest. Life was good. But things quickly got even better.

On December 26th, 2011, less than a month after listing my software for sale on Warrior Forum, I woke up and checked my emails immediately, the same as I did every morning. Today was different. Instead of a few emails here and there, I had hundreds. As I scrolled through them, almost half said "SALE NOTIFICATION." There were dozens of support requests, and everything was chaotic and confusing. I snapped out of my slumber instantly. What the hell was going on?

As it turns out, my product had received an awarded dubbed the "Warrior Special Offer of the Day." When your product looks promising to affiliates (in terms of conversion and earning stats), the affiliate network of the forum chooses your product and promotes it to the entire forum as the "Product of the Day." In essence, the forum itself is the largest affiliate, and blesses one product owner with incredible affiliate sales for one day. December 26th, 2011 was my day. I brought in over $10,000 worth of sales during those 24 hours, and got another unexpected bump when I was featured as the "Warrior Special Offer of the Week" a few days afterwards.

I spent that entire day furiously responding to emails and creating licenses for each new customer. Sales continued to flow after the 26th, but gradually came down to a more manageable pace. I went back for the second semester of school, and when I was on break during early February, I received some of the worst news I have ever received in the history of my business ventures.

The events of the day will be burned in my memory for a long time. I was sitting on a patio in Florida with my family. It was a nice day out. We had just woken up. My phone made a noise and I saw an email from PayPal. The subject line was "Your account has been limited until we hear from you." My heart stopped. I had heard about PayPal limitations, but never thought it would happen to me.

When PayPal limits your account, you can't send or receive payments. My cash flow was cut off completely. New licenses could not be purchased and my monthly customers couldn't pay me, either. Remember how I said that offering a lifetime license option was a mistake? I stand by that, but due to sheer misfortune, my mistake turned out to benefit me. All of my recurring customers were essentially canceled, but I had built up a decent bankroll because of the lump-sum purchases, which turned out to be a very handy safety net.

Still, it was a bad situation overall, and the next incident with PayPal support made it turn from bad to worse. I called the listed number and the representative on the other end told me politely that there was absolutely nothing he could do to help me.

At this point, you may be wondering why PayPal closed my account. It makes sense, but there's no way I could have seen it coming. I sold about 1,000 licenses of software in a short time, and about 50 people requested refunds through the dispute system on PayPal. Some customers were unsatisfied with how it took me a day to set up the license, whereas others exploited the system and demanded a refund even after having access to the software. My refund rate was 5%, which is low in the world of internet marketing products. But to a standard payment process, a refund rate of 5%—technically a chargeback rate, because these customers used the PayPal dispute system instead of contacting me directly—is quite high. So PayPal limited the account. Back around 2011, PayPal was notorious for doing stuff like this.

I was forced to act fast. My coder was justifiably threatening to stop working without payment, and bug reports were coming in every day. I had 1,000 users and the software needed to work if I wanted to keep them happy. I ended up getting a Payoneer card, which is sort of like a prepaid Mastercard. I combined that with 2Checkout, another payment processor similar to PayPal. 2Checkout accepted the payments for the software, then deposited the money into my payoneer account, which I could then use to send money to my programmer. This approach turned out to be a decent stopgap solution, but 2Checkout also closed my account in time as well, presumably for the same reasons as PayPal.

My next stop was Clickbank, a payment processor known for the vast number of affiliates that use it to find new products to promote. It's a huge company—over 200 million customers worldwide and over $1 billion in payments processed. Clickbank was easy to get set up, but their fees are outrageous, and between splitting the sales with affiliates and paying the Clickbank fees, I was earning far less per sale than I had hoped. I needed to get back to PayPal.

In order to get my PayPal account back, I knew I had to be resourceful. The official support was giving me no help, but still, I was a real customer who processed real amounts of money, and they had thrown me under the bus. At this point, lots of companies had started using social media to handle support requests from the public, and I saw that as my "in." They replied to requests within minutes—a stark contrast from the email support, which took days to send you a templated message. Because I had almost 1,000 followers on Twitter, I felt confident I could get a reply.

I tweeted something along the lines of "@PayPal I processed tens of thousands of dollars with you and you guys treat me like this?" To my surprise, the official PayPal account replied to me within minutes, and after 12 months of having my account closed, I was able to have my case reviewed, and my account reopened. Recovering a limited account was very rare, and is still quite rare to this day, but my strategy ended up working. Sometimes I still laugh about how a single Tweet did infinitely more than my countless emails and phone calls had over the course of a year.

So I had my account back, but I didn't have my recurring customers back. Those were still gone. Too bad, so sad. Some customers re-subscribed, but not enough, and the sales on Clickbank had slowed to a trickle, too. The monthly revenue just kept dropping. I was losing my motivation. I could have added new features, but I knew doing that wouldn't bring the sales back, and I would just be dumping money into a dead project. So, I decided to maintain the software for the remaining months, to honor my promise to my paying customers. Eventually, my software became outdated, as the internet marketing industry moves at a blinding pace. My customers jumped to the next big thing and Keyword Scout was finished.

At one point, I made a connection with a man named Todd Gross, and we partnered to release a cheaper version of Keyword Scout with fewer features, called Keyword Scout Lite. The launch was successful, but sales dropped off eventually, and it wasn't worth continuing. (Todd Gross used to be a meteorologist before becoming a successful internet marketer. I remember seeing him cover Hurricane Sandy in 2015 on CNBC. Anyone, no matter what your background is, can make it in this industry.)

The other day, I had a friend reveal to me that he was thinking of shooting me an offer to buy Keyword Scout from me when it was popular, which reminded me of something. Another friend *had* offered $35,000 to buy me out when sales were steady, but I had turned the offer down. I consider this to be a good decision, as I ended up earning more than $35,000 in the long run. The memory does cause me some remorse, though. If PayPal had not canceled my account, and if I had kept the recurring model, I believe I could have reached 250 monthly customers at $39.99 each fairly easily, which is about $10,000 every month. The programmer was about $1,000 per month, so that was $9,000 of profit every month, and software companies with recurring customers are usually valued at roughly 30x the monthly profit—in my case, $270,000. If I had done everything correctly and had perfect luck, my life might be much different than it is today. But I can't complain. Keyword Scout was overall a massive success and the first stepping stone to my life today.

Slowly, Keyword Scout developed the reputation of being "closed for business" as intended, but I kept circling back to the success I had found on that particular project. I had the idea to develop a new keyword tool, named Keyword Tycoon. I would completely rebrand the tool, change the pricing structure, add new features, and move existing customers over free of charge... then the thought began to overwhelm me, which confused me at first. Keyword Scout was huge for me. Why didn't I want to continue on that same path?

When I thought about it, I realized I was facing internal resistance when I thought of the new project because I was sick and tired of selling keyword research tools. The money was good, but the stress was immense, especially with such limited time as a high school student. I'll give you one example. A certain function broke during math class, which rendered the tool basically useless. Immediately, customer complaints started piling up. I had to look at the clock, convert it to Indian Standard Time, think how long it would take my programmer to fix things, then get back to all of my customers as quickly as possible, all while, you know, being in school. This scenario happened weekly, as the program relied on a myriad of third-party data sources. At least one of these sources would make some sort of modification to its data structures every week, which would prompt that anxiety-inducing process described above.

The decision was made. There were too many unreliable data sources that I was forced to incorporate into my software... despite my success, I would never, ever, go back into keyword tools. I've seen this type of attitude frequently, and from what I've found, it encompasses success of all types. Even if you see success in something, once you've seen the inner workings of the industry, you might recommend against it. I recommend against creating keyword research tools. Too much time, too much stress. (On a positive note, I knew the skills cultivated from creating and maintaining Keyword Scout would transfer to another project in the future.)

All throughout high school, during Keyword Scout and beyond, I kept my close friends up to date on what I was working on. One of my friends, Justin Kowalsky, was usually equally as bored as I was during class. We talked about my projects all of the time. Once, we planned a website for people to submit and rate trucks, called "Rate That Rig" (trucks were immensely popular in the small town I grew up in), but it never came to fruition because we could not think of how to monetize it. Many of these ideas between friends were had, but despite our commonalities, I ended up always doing business either by myself or with another business-oriented person from the internet. Maybe it was better that way.

Something young people reading this book need to understand is that your biggest obstacle will be your focus when you are thinking of your ideas. It's not all fun, but you can't let that stop you. Thinking of your vision and hiring a developer to turn it into a reality is a blast. But there are also administrative headaches like customer support, payment processing, as well as marketing aspects like sales page and email opt-in pages, etc. I've noticed that the younger you are, the quicker you give up and move onto the next project, only to hit the same roadblocks yet again. Older people do tend to have more focus and not jump around as much, but the focus problem rings true for everyone, even the most experienced. Be aware of it.

Since Keyword Scout, I continued my education at Queen's University, then the University of Toronto, after being diagnosed with Crohn's disease and wanting to be closer to home. During that time, I started new software ventures like SerpClix, as well as various business ventures like ShoutOurBiz.

The remainder of the book will consist of me giving you my exact process that I use to turn my ideas into real, tangible successes. I'll also be giving you close to a decade of raw first-hand experience that will be invaluable to you when you start yourself.

PART 1

• • • • • • • •

The Ideation Stage

I would say the biggest misunderstanding [that non-technical people have about starting a software company] is probably that it's easier than people think. The biggest hurdle I see from non-technical founders is the feeling of inferiority. You know, "I don't understand this stuff, therefore, I can't get it done." And yet we see this every day. Lots of people come to Upwork and have great ideas but they don't know how to get it done and are looking for people that will help them get it done. This happens millions of times per year and you know the success rate is extremely high. Probably the biggest thing is debunking the myth that you need to have a PhD in computer science to build a mobile app or launch a website or any of that. What you really need is to have a good idea, understand what the market needs and be able to find great people to find great people to help you execute the idea.

STEPHANE KASRIEL

CEO, UPWORK

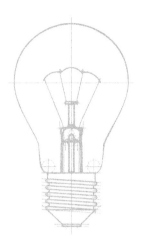

CHAPTER 1

• • • • • • • •

HOW TO THINK OF AN IDEA

M aybe you have an idea for a piece of software you'd like to develop. Maybe you don't. If you do have an idea, you probably think that it's the best idea and that it's better than anyone else's idea. You think that you just need a programmer to put it together, and you'll be rich. (I've heard this story too many times.)

I think the issue is that some people get so excited by entrepreneurship that they start too early and in the end it discourages them from actually continuing as an entrepreneur. If you experience failure or if you have a few really bad failures a lot of people say "oh failures motivate you! You need to fail" but if you have tremendous amount of super bad failures then they'll like totally discourage you. If you're interested in being an entrepreneur make it a plan. So, say I want to be an entrepreneur in this industry but before I do that let me take a job, an internship, let me take courses, let me learn about this industry. A lot of times once you do that a year into the industry, you realize this is much harder than it looks or this is like pretty low barrier of entry business that I might start so my competition's going to be heavy, stuff of that sort. Try to learn about industry very strongly because to be an entrepreneur you're going to have to have a lot of passion and you're going to have to wake up every morning thinking about it and fighting through it, through weekends and holidays. So if you're not super motivated about it then you're not going to be successful.

DAVID MARKOVICH

FOUNDER, ONLINE GENIUSES

Ideas are Worthless Without Proper Execution

The #1 misconception most people have about software is that the best idea wins. Let me be clear: a solid idea with user interest is vital. But if you put together a group of highly-talented, passionate individuals who are working towards a single goal, they will change the direction of the first idea at will to make it work. Instagram actually started as an app called Burbn, which is nothing like the Instagram we know today.

"Burbn let users check in at particular locations, make plans for future check-ins, earn points for hanging out with friends, and post pictures of the meet-ups," reported Megan Garber of The Atlantic. Soon after launch, the team at Burbn realized that most people were using the app to primarily share photos, so in late 2010, they relaunched Burbn as Instagram.

The world likes to find a hero who ideally works in a basement somewhere and came up with this brilliant idea and then the world changed. I have sympathy for the human desire to fit things in that mold but I believe that is not how innovation happens. I think innovation is much more a product of different people working together and coming up with stuff. It doesn't happen within a single individual, it happens between people. We just have this undeniable desire to create heroes. It's our part of our human god genes.

We love to create heroes and we love to think of gods. It's just sort of in our nature. I think fundamentally that's not how it really happens.

FRANK VAN MIERLO

FOUNDER, 1366 TECHNOLOGIES

Once you have an idea—any idea at all—you should test it in a number of different ways to determine if it is viable or not. You can't judge the idea yourself, especially if this is your first attempt at creating software. You will probably guess wrong. Luckily, there are certain procedures you can follow to objectively determine if your idea is viable. We will get to those soon.

Once you validate your idea, you must execute the idea. You can't sit on it. If the idea is any good, someone else will think of it and execute it before you do. I've seen hugely successful projects on Kickstarter and said to myself, "I thought of that first." Maybe you have, too. It's not a nice feeling.

Understand now that ideas are worth nothing until executed. Zip. Zero. Zilch! Derek Sivers says it best…

Ideas are just a multiplier of execution

It's so funny when I hear people being so protective of ideas. (People who want me to sign an NDA to tell me the simplest idea.) To me, ideas are worth nothing unless executed. They are just a multiplier. Execution is worth millions:

Awful idea =	-1	No execution =	$1
Weak idea =	1	Weak execution =	$1,000
So-so idea =	5	So-so execution =	$10,000
Good idea =	10	Good execution =	$100,000
Great idea =	15	Great execution =	$1,000,000
Brilliant idea =	20	Brilliant execution =	$10,000,000

To make a business, you need to multiply the two.
The most brilliant idea, with no execution, is worth $20.
The most brilliant idea takes great execution to be worth $20,000,000.
That's why I don't want to hear people's ideas.
I'm not interested until I see their execution.

Derek Sivers (sivers.org)
Originally posted on Oreillynet.com, August 16, 2005

Ideas are Just a Multiplier of Execution

Paul Graham once wrote an essay that covered why some people think coming up with ideas is hard. In truth, the average entrepreneur comes up with several ideas every single month, and possibly more. Graham found the issue to be that the majority of people see successful companies and assume they are successful *because of an awesome idea*. They think the founders of that company were the very first people to think of an idea!

That's rarely the case. Ideas are plentiful. You might think you have the best idea ever, but you can't even determine if the idea is good by yourself (more on that soon). Use this newfound understanding of ideas to keep your sanity during your first projects.

> *I did not have much of an intention to start 87 AM. I had another job in Hollywood as a talent manager and I relocated from Los Angeles to New York for personal reasons but retained the job I had in LA. Long story short the company I worked for ran into a financial snag, structured and I lost my job, so I needed a job. I think I submitted 600 resumes for a first interview and I didn't get one of them. So I needed something to do and that's how the company came about. It was not some strong business plan that came about. It wasn't a 'when I was 12, I wanted to be a CEO'—it was never part of the plan. It's just what happened.*
>
> **ADAM CUNNINGHAM**
> *FOUNDER, 87AM*

Now you are aware that the average beginner egregiously overvalues ideas, and you can stop being so protective of your idea! No one cares, and if they do, they almost certainly do not have the knowledge or resources to act on it.

You may have heard of NDAs (non-disclosure agreements). They are contracts that both parties sign to confirm they will not share or act on the ideas presented. In essence, these contracts are how adults say "I won't tell, I swear!" but with potential legal repercussions. Most beginners think they need one of these before they talk with an investor, because the idea is so incredibly valuable they cannot take any risks. If you actually manage to meet an investor and you ask for him to sign a NDA before speaking, he won't care, and he will disregard you entirely like he does to thousands of other aspiring entrepreneurs every single year. He knows your idea is worthless without proper execution, and he won't waste his time on you.

> *You know what's interesting? Practically nobody asks us to sign one. If they do, we laugh and kick them out.*
>
> **SANJAY SINGHAL**
>
> *CANADIAN VENTURE PARTNER, 500 STARTUPS*

Instead, if you meet a potential investor or partner, just pitch the basics of your idea, whatever is needed get the point across, in roughly 15 seconds. If you manage to catch the interest of the other party, then you might think about asking to sign the NDA. You need to be able to catch interest before you are seen as someone worthy of asking for a NDA, though. You can use this same pitch to tell other people about your project in a satisfactory manner without talking their ears off.

I know, I know. You're scared the investor will run off with the idea, but that will very rarely happen. For one, investors don't have time for that, and even if they did, it would be difficult to find someone like you who is the brains powering the idea. Do you think a non-committed investor could have stolen the idea of Facebook and tried to compete with Mark Zuckerberg? I don't think so. Maybe they could have made a replica, but as the mastermind, Zuckerberg would have quickly evolved to defeat them, in ways they could not think of without the mastermind helping them.

There are certain cases when talking about your idea might come back to bite you. If you mention anything to a competitor, like if I mentioned a new feature of Keyword Scout to another keyword research product owner, he might race to implement the feature before me. As another example, if I had a new software idea but I was hanging around with software developers exactly like myself, I might not mention the specifics. If someone has the time and resources to take your idea, he might take it. But these types of situations are rare. Don't be scared to talk to friends and family about your idea, assuming they fall outside of the above criteria.

Now you know the basics of the ideas as a whole. Next, we will talk about where you should get your ideas. Some people can come up with their own ideas, but in the case that you haven't, or you don't think your ideas are any good, we will discuss a few bulletproof sources of ideas that you can call on at any time.

Listening to Friends and Family

The first way you can get ideas is by listening to your family and your friends. People love to tell you their ideas, because most of the time they have absolutely no intention of acting on them whatsoever. This strategy is good for coming up with broad ideas, but less useful when it comes to software development, because most of your friends and family are (probably) not thinking of new app and software ideas every day, and even if they are, technologically-challenged people usually have no idea what the limits of technology are; meaning their super-awesome ideas are usually wholly unrealistic.

Our CEO, Rick Perreault, had two ideas, this was back in 2009, and a whole group of us, maybe 10, sat around to debate them and agreed this was the better of the two. Then eventually, it whittled down to 6 of us, we have 6 co-founders.

OLI GARDNER

CO-FOUNDER, UNBOUNCE

Use Your Personal Experience

With Keyword Scout, I built what I needed. I knew I needed a better keyword tool than what I could find on the market, so I made one. As luck had it, many other people needed the same thing. This phenomenon tends to hold true across all types of ideas—if you have a use for it, other people probably do, too. If you are using any products right now, start there. If you feel that a certain product is overpriced or lacking in features, maybe it's something you should consider.

With this method of idea generation, you understand the idea in full. You know exactly what is needed, and exactly why it is needed. For a non-programmer, knowing these things is ideal, because it's difficult to envision what is possible if you haven't done it before. If there are already competing products on the market, you already know with near certainty that you can develop something similar.

> *I had been using Xenu for years to help with auditing websites and analyzing them to make informed SEO recommendations for clients. It was a great crawler (and still is), but it wasn't focused enough on SEO.*
>
> *So, we built something for us as an agency to help. It was a problem that needed solving. We then realized others might like it, too.*
>
> **DAN SHARP**
>
> *FOUNDER, SCREAMING FROG*

> *We built a product that we needed. Right before Hotjar came out on the market, most tools I was using as part of my role were expensive and complicated. You had to pay for a year or you had to speak to a sales team and you needed multiple tools in order to get the job done. So, it was kind of a pain for us and I think that's why we got such a great reaction from so many other people when we launched the Hotjar preview.*
>
> **DR. DAVID DARMANIN**
>
> *CO-FOUNDER, HOTJAR*

> *It's a cliché to say but only because it's so true: you really should focus on solving problems that you have. And it always seems that way, too. Products*

that do the best are the ones where the founders had a problem they needed to resolve and they built the tool for themselves, not necessarily thinking about other people and it took off. You know we had one client with $20,000,000 in funding called Genymotion, out in Paris. And Genymotion started out as an Android app development company. That's what they were doing, they were an agency. They had a problem where it was really hard for them to develop apps because they would code, code, code and then they would have to forward it out to an Android phone to actually test it or they would have to use one of the existing testing solutions, which were really slow. So they actually took a month or two of their own time and built a better Android testing environment; like a place where you could run your Android apps to figure out how well they worked and then put it up for free. They put it on GitHub or something like that so everyone could try it… And it exploded. Like hundreds of thousands of people started using it because it was the best thing on the market and the next thing you know they're pivoting away from being an agency and directly into this. It was now their product. There are so many stories like that of people who wanted something to solve this problem for themselves and it just kind of blew up into something they didn't expect. You see all kinds of startups come through. Like for every client we take on there are 4 others that are just horrible ideas we don't take on and I feel like there's a lot of people who try to force it. They put the idea "I want to be an entrepreneur" and "I want to have a product before the conceptualization of what that's gonna be" and try to force something. I definitely think people want this kind of thing, but then shocked to find out they don't. If it wasn't a problem for you, why would it be a problem for anybody else? If you go on tech websites like TechCrunch, you'll see a lot of stupid ideas thrown out around there. Even if it gets funding, it doesn't mean that it's not stupid.

ILAN NASS

FOUNDER, TAKTICAL DIGITAL

A little over 4 years ago I was working at the agency in New York as I mentioned and was doing some of my own side consulting. Basically got to the point where I realized that I was 27-28-years-old, living in Brooklyn, single, and spending two weekends a month in my apartment by myself, doing work for clients, making money that I didn't need. Decided I wanted to have less stress in my life, so I told my clients I was going to stop consulting at the end of that year and they started asking me who they should work with. I didn't have a good answer. I was pretty well-known in the SEO world and had other people coming to me wanting to work with me. I ended up building a Google spreadsheet of people I knew they could work with and started sending work to them. I realized that, huh, people actually paid for leads. So, I got a project I knew would be perfect for my buddy and it was in his hometown. I pinged my buddy Brandon and said, "hey, man, I got this project. Would you be willing to pay 50 bucks for the intro?" and he replied, "yeah, what's your PayPal?" Three minutes later, I had 50 bucks in my PayPal account. I sent him the intro and was like huh, maybe there's something here. I bought a domain, threw it up on some shared hosting that I had. It very much started from my own necessity. I just kind of worked a little bit over the next few years as I went in-house, got married, got a dog and moved a couple times but it was constantly on my mind that I wanted to do more with it. I didn't know if it was a marketplace or a platform or a media company or what it was. But I knew there was something there and I knew it was something people wanted so it just stayed on my mind.

JOHN DOHERTY

FOUNDER, CREDO

Read Industry Forums

My preferred type of software is B2B (business-to-business), built for a specific industry—software that manages the inventory of a car dealership, software that manages dental office bookings, or software that routes trucks across the country. There is the potential for big money with this particular type of software. In every industry, software already exists that you can scout

out to see if there is any potential for feature improvements or additional value.

In the industry of search engine optimization, there are different forums where marketers hang around and discuss, amongst other things, the software they are using and looking for. You can find entire threads that discuss what is available on the market and what is missing from those offerings. This information is invaluable when deciding on an idea.

These industry forums also provide another valuable tool: interested people to use as your beta testers. Your beta testers can give you valuable insight into your product and help you with bug fixes before you open it up to the masses. And, they turn into customers—if someone enjoys the beta of a product, he will frequently buy the full version when it is released.

Find a problem you are curious about learning more about, and try to find all the issues around it. Eventually, while you poke and prod around a specific industry, you will find plenty of opportunity for startup ideas. However, don't say "I'm going to start a company," you should be saying, "I'm going to solve a problem in X sector" and then you hope the problem impacts enough people to make a sustainable company.

ADAM DRAPER
FOUNDER, BOOST VC

Read Industry News

Beginners often look at the news, see a successful startup like Uber, and start thinking about how to replicate something like it. That's not a particularly healthy approach to generating your idea, but the news in any industry can be a valuable source of creative inspiration. The mainstream articles talking about billion-dollar rounds of investing are interesting to read, but we are more interested in the articles talking about brand-new companies that are young (6 months to a year).

Websites like TechCrunch and VentureBeat do a good job covering new startups that show promise. CrunchBase is another resource you will want to look at. CrunchBase maintains a list of every company to receive funding.

I like looking at the seed investment funding, as that cuts through all of the bigger companies and shows you who is getting investments for the first time.

If you subscribe to the CrunchBase newsletter, you can watch ideas jump from $50k in funding, to $1m, all the way to $5m and beyond, simply because they were included in the newsletter and readers took notice. Getting investment isn't impossible. See what investors are interested in and adapt your approach to follow what is working.

I like to think of Seed/Series A/Series B in a perfect world, like you would the scientific method. First you come up with an idea, and attempt it on your own. When you have gotten far enough to prove you know the market and believe you have an opportunity, you can raise money to prove or disprove your hypothesis, but ideally learn from it and find an opportunity. When you have figured out how the opportunity works, and you have been paid for the service, the Series A is the round you need to take the hypothesis you proved and repeat the process a lot to figure out how big the market gets, if you see no end in sight then raise a B round to own the market.

ADAM DRAPER

FOUNDER, BOOST VC

Speak with the Younger Generations

College students are early adopters. Understand that college students, and sometimes high school students, drive many trends. Over in America, students started wearing Hollister and UGG Boots as trends. The trend spread to adults, where it then died. This is a common pattern when we talk about trends in general. Students start the trends; adults kill the trends.

Technology especially! As we all know, Facebook started out on college campuses. Yik Yak, Tinder, and Snapchat are also products of the younger audience, most of which began on college campuses. These websites and apps start on the campus breeding grounds and expand to older audiences from there.

Gary Vaynerchuk is one of the people who gets it. He is constantly seeking out the things that youth is interested in. When Musically, a video social app, was launched, he jumped on it quickly, even though it was just another app to most people. I highly recommend Gary Vaynerchuk to everyone reading this book. As an introduction, his video series "Ask GaryVee," is him answering user-submitted questions, which is a fantastic resource for idea generation.

Beat an Existing Option

A company like Stripe might have sounded foolish when it was originally pitched, considering the tight stranglehold PayPal had on the market at the time. But Stripe excelled where PayPal was weak, and turned itself into a multi-billion dollar company, and direct competitor to PayPal, despite launching a full 12 years after PayPal did. Facebook wasn't the first social network. Tesla, valued at over $50 billion, wasn't the first car manufacturer, or even the first company to explore electric vehicles. If your idea is based on current market options, you will have a much easier time convincing others of your idea's merit. "Double selling"—convincing someone both that he has a problem, and that he needs your product to fix the problem—is quite difficult.

Consider the task of trying to sell Apple Music to a man in his 60s. He doesn't know that he needs a service like Apple Music. You explain the curated playlists, and he asks why he needs curated playlists when he has his FM radio that plays all of the music he wants. This man does not have a problem. You will have to convince him that his current music setup is lackluster before you begin trying to sell him on Apple Music, which is utterly exhausting.

Now consider trying to sell hot dogs out of a stand that is 100 feet away from a nightclub. People come out of the nightclub, and they are hungry. They walk to your hot dog stand because they have a problem, and you are there to solve it with your product. You didn't have to convince them they were hungry... they already knew that, and they were looking for a solution when you came into the picture. That's a lot easier than trying to convince someone his trusty FM radio, is, in fact, subpar.

We were creating a free and open alternative to Adobe's similar product. So that was the first mission. What we're doing is we're trying to make something that's really flexible for developers that allows them to build upon much easier than what Adobe had provided. And also, it is cheaper for sure. Especially when it's free, open source; that's way cheaper. The pro version is a licensed model. It's built on top of the open source code so we still contribute back to the open source but there are modules that sit on top that enable kind of high scalability through a very sophisticated clustering model.

CHRIS ALLEN

CO-FOUNDER, RED5

Talk to People in the Industry

We continue to focus on industry because sources within any industry are the best resource for discovering ideas for a product. I touched on industry forums briefly, and while industry forums are incredibly valuable, they may not always exist. If you need to reach Fortune 500 executives, they're probably not hanging around on any forums.

Let's say you want to build a piece of software for the marketing industry, and you are looking to talk to marketing agency managers to find out what problems they are having. When you reach out to them, your goal is to find out about any hardships they are experiencing regarding your area of interest, but without asking directly or coming off too strongly. If you can strike a balance, you get totally unbiased information, which will be brimming with ideas for you to consider. Remember, you're not selling anything here. You're just asking questions. You can ask things like:

What service are you using to accomplish what you need currently? If they are using nothing, that might mean there is no demand. If they are using a full-service solution, there may not be room in the market for someone new like you. If they are using something in between, you may have a thread to follow.

How much are you paying? If the current solution has a high price point, maybe your edge can be undercutting that. If the price point seems too low, remember that if you make a higher-priced version, you will need to convince the customer that your solution is well worth the extra money.

What's missing? You can learn about potential new features, and if you have the attention of whoever you are asking, this question can often lead you to more valuable information, and possibly down a path you hadn't even considered before.

Have you ever used the customer support? How did you feel about it? Maybe the current solution offers only phone support, when the company would strongly prefer to use a live chat interface. Every small advantage you can give yourself over a current solution is worth taking note of.

Any bugs in your current solution? In more traditional industries, you will find that the leading industry software is often clunky, outdated, and filled to the brim with all sorts of bugs. Ask this question and whoever you are asking will be happy to complain to you. Just let them talk. Don't be pushy, or you risk creating bias and tainting your understanding of the industry.

> *I have a friend of mine—we were on vacation last week and he came up with an idea for a dating app and he pitched it to me from the van, sitting in front of me. It was interesting. Okay that's cool, we moved onto something else and I called him up and said, "hey can we get together?" I showed him all the work I'd done advancing the idea, finding somebody to actually run the company designing a minimum viable product, finding some workspace and he was like "Holy shit! You did all this in 5 days?! I thought that was just a random conversation we had." And I said, "No dude, what role do you wanna have? It's your idea." "No I was just throwing ideas around, I don't wanna have a role. Include me in the brainstorming, cause it's kind of fun." Now, most people are like him. There's not many entrepreneurs out there.*
>
> **SANJAY SINGHAL**
> *CANADIAN VENTURE PARTNER, 500 STARTUPS*

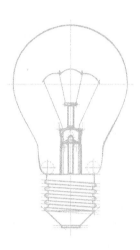

CHAPTER 2

• • • • • • • •

HOW TO VALIDATE AN IDEA

You do your idea generation and you decide on an idea you believe to be "good." But what's a good idea? Lots of beginners think that a good idea is any idea for a product or service that people will use. It's not as simple as that. A good idea is any idea that you can prove will produce both demand and profitability.

Many budding entrepreneurs settle on an idea they think is good initially… then fail to adapt when they are proven wrong. This path leads to headaches, and quite frankly, despair. Most of your ideas will be flops, and you don't want to spend time or money on something bound to flop. Instead, before starting, you should first attempt to determine if your idea is viable with the highest degree of certainty possible. The following text explains how to do just that.

Looking back, Demio was a technical challenge especially at the time. The actual idea itself, in some ways, had already been validated. We had our unique proposition and we talked to a few people about that. We didn't by any means go through and have a ton of interviews. Luckily for us though we were would-be customers of our own product. So, we were solving our own problems. Not only that, but at the time and to this day, there was an influx of social media posts about how bad the current solutions were.

WYATT JOZWOWSKI
CO-FOUNDER, DEMIO

Don't Ask Family and Friends

Attempting to validate ideas is human nature. You want confirmation that an idea is good before you act on it. You likely have already developed ways of trying to validate your ideas, likely by accident. An extremely common go-to idea validation method is asking friends and family what they think about an idea. Getting a second opinion is smart—it prevents you from developing tunnel vision—but at the same time, friends and family are an awful place to get a second opinion. They will be biased in your favor, or possibly against it if they can't relate to your ambitions. Some family members may be able to give you a good second opinion, but you will get more realistic feedback when you are certain the person you are asking is not afraid to tell you your idea sucks.

Try to find someone neutral to bounce your ideas off of. That person is not your mother, who will be biased in your favor, nor your Aunt Cindy, who thinks the internet is a big scam, and will be biased against it. You are looking for someone who has no real interest in you or your well-being or success.

When I was thinking about writing this book, the majority of my friends and family encouraged me to do it, as I am lucky to have positive people in my life. But, that encouragement had a limited effect on my decision, as I knew they were biased in my favor. The turning point was when random connections and acquaintances started bothering me for early access after I mentioned my idea for the book. The unbiased crowd wanted it; that's the moment I knew the book was a good idea.

There are certain fringe cases where a friend or family member can be a big help. If someone close to you is in the same industry and has access to investment capital, by all means, talk to him and potentially work with him. But that scenario won't apply to the vast majority of readers, so as a general guideline, stay far away from friends and family when you are trying to validate an idea. If you have been using friends and family for idea validation already, you may have to make a conscious effort to stop doing so.

> *For a while, there was on the part of investors, such desperation to not miss out to the point that they were showering money on everybody just to see what would happen. And so people with poor ideas and maybe great personal skills and good connections could manage to raise funding. Funding has become this sort of validation point in our industry, where if you get funding that's when you matter, no matter what. Like even if you suck. 'Oh we raised funds, so we're good at what we do.' It doesn't necessarily mean that you're validated, it just means someone believed in you. I've seen it all. I still see it and it hasn't stopped but it's reduced a lot. Now it's a lot harder to raise money unless you have some sort of proof that your idea is real.*

ILAN NASS

FOUNDER, TAKTICAL DIGITAL

Build a Team

A recent study conducted by FirstRound.com found that teams of founders outperformed solo founders by 163%. Solopreneurs were valued 25% less than average, compared to projects which has more than one founder. You can certainly do it yourself. But finding a partner or a team to work with can be incredibly beneficial when validating your idea. It's one thing to have your friends say you have a good idea. It's quite another to have someone pour their time, money, heart, and soul into your project because he believes in the potential that much. A partner, or a team, can also help you judge your idea accurately, as well as any decision you make moving forward.

The Minimum Viable Product

Your end goal is to sell a piece of software. But you can only predict so much on paper. Your MVP is a basic version of your idea, with all of the bells and whistles stripped off. Once you have your MVP you can start trying to sell it and validate your idea even further. For some ideas, creating a MVP is easy, for others, it is incredibly difficult.

The idea of a minimum viable product is, at this point, gospel. The idea of going out and building a gigantic product that has all these features, first of all, if you're not a developer it's going to cost you a hell of a lot. If you hire someone to do the job for you it's going to be an astronomical expense. And it's going to break and it's not going to work well and you're going to change things because you don't really know what people are going to want. Like you don't know what future people are going to like. I think there's a social network that started off as a social network for musicians or something like that, and then they pivoted, right. Because they built one feature that blew up and now they're like okay this is the product now. So you have to sort of start somewhere with the basic idea and grow from there and I think the perfect example of this is Snapchat. Where the premise of the app is that kids were being told, "listen you can't post these kinds of pictures. You can't. You know these pictures are gonna get around someone's gonna copy it, someone's gonna screenshot it" and they said yeah well we'll just have photos that disappear. It didn't have chat, it didn't have stories, it didn't have timers it didn't have filters. It didn't have anything. It was very simple. You send a picture and it disappears. It didn't even have the ability to control how long the picture would be there. Just send a picture and it disappears. That's it. And from there they were able to build out all the features after and test what works and what didn't once they had a critical mass.

ILAN NASS

FOUNDER, TAKTICAL DIGITAL

Facebook is a good example to use because everyone understands the features of Facebook. When Facebook was launched, its features were simplistic. You could only fill out your profile, add friends, and message them. You didn't even have a "wall," which we now consider an essential part of Facebook. The founders really didn't spend a lot of time on it. Instead, they created a MVP with barebones features and proceeded to try to get users. Once Facebook caught on, the founders saw that their MVP had worked, and rushed to add more features to turn it into the robust platform it is today. Almost every big idea in the world today can be stripped down to its core functions.

Once you create your MVP, you will be able to show it to potential customers, along with a short sales pitch, and be able to fully convey what your idea is to them. Then, they can make the decision to buy or not, and with each decision you learn more about the potential of your idea.

> *If the product is really simple, say it takes a weekend to build the MVP, share it around and that's it, it's copied. So, like a chrome extension, like a really simple chrome extension or a simple Slack bot. I think that's the only case where I'd say don't build an MVP. If it's so simple and you know the barrier of entry is really small. If you built an MVP and shared it around, somebody will actually just be able to do it.*

DAVID MARKOVICH

FOUNDER, ONLINE GENIUSES

Identify Your Customer

Facebook doesn't have paying users. They make their money from servings ads to their users. This business model is a sharp contrast to a company like Netflix, which sells to consumers, or a company like Oracle, which sells enterprise computing solutions to businesses.

Regardless of the business model, the first step is always identifying your customer category, which is simple. Will you be selling to business, or consumers? If you are selling to businesses, you are B2B, and if you are selling to consumers, you are B2C. Most businesses you can think of off the top of your head are B2C, but don't let that scare you from pursuing B2B projects.

Ever watched the Golf Channel? You'll see commercials for companies where you can't tell what the company even does. You don't see any value from the commercial because you are watching the golf channel as a consumer, whereas those ads are targeting B2B customers; many of whom just happen to watch the Golf Channel.

As an extreme example of this, think about Oracle, an absolutely massive and very successful B2B company. You probably can't name three products they offer. Maybe you can't name a single one! That's because you are not the B2B customer they want to reach, and they do a very good job with their ad targeting. Once you know who your customer is, you have the information you need to figure out how to reach him.

We love startups using our product but they're not our target market. We want them to talk about us. They can use for validation and experimentation but our target market is in-house marketing teams and agencies, and also the people who use PPC, because that has a strong tie to landing pages. It gives us a 4x value when we have the people that do that.

It can take a long time to discover your ideal customer and when do find it, that's the most important thing. When you discover that, you drive all your content and marketing at those specific people. That's kind of the tipping point when you figure out the lifetime value and who that comes from.

It's all done with analytics. This bunch of customers are staying with us longer or they're upgrading, etc. It can be tough because you have to connect systems in the back end to be able to actually access that data. We did a lot of work. Our data team connecting all the systems, from our billing systems into product usage and a lot of different things. It can be difficult to figure that out as we only figured it out within the past year.

OLI GARDNER
CO-FOUNDER, UNBOUNCE

Business-to-Business

B2B is my preferred type of customer. I prefer fewer sales and large transactions over a higher number of sales and smaller transactions. Let's say your goal is to earn $100,000 per year. Ignoring expenses, to earn $10,000 every month, you could sell a $10 product to 1,000 people, or you could sell a $1,000 product to 10 companies. Which one sounds more appealing? Both are good options. Different people will prefer one or the other. For example, one of the reasons I prefer B2B is because you develop intimate relationships with a small number of people, rather than shallow relationships with thousands of people. You may prefer it the other way around.

> *Formerly I was president of a small, publicly traded company. We were selling electronic prescribing software and we had negotiated North American rights for a device that was offshore. This was similar to what you call a POS credit card receiving device, and you signed your signature. We would do some emancipations on how it would be developed and how you could compare one to an earlier enrollment for example.*
>
> *So we were sitting in front of the DEA in the United States. They were concerned about electronic scribing for controlled substances. That's all your pain meds and other products on the black market and a lot of people are hooked on called opioids. They were looking at our product and said this is very good but this particular unit is way too expensive for our 600,000 physicians. Each physician needs, you know, 3 or 4 different types of it. The price of it was just way out of whack and they said "can you come back and develop a software biometric because that would be what we would be looking for without the use of any special hardware?" So it was one of those epiphany moments when I looked at my Vietnamese CTO and I said "uh do you think you can help me build this?" and he said, "yeah, I think we can." That started the odyssey of creating this software biometric and all of the mechanisms that went into it, such as researching the market, researching who to do this development work, all the marketing and sales, how to become an expert and so forth.*
>
> **JEFF MAYNARD**
> *PRESIDENT AND CEO, BIOMETRIC SIGNATURE ID*

If you sell software to companies, you will need to sign contracts, and you will need to offer real security. Imagine your software handles sensitive company data and someone manages to hack their way in. Executives could be fired and investors could lose money. The company could get horribly negative press. In return, the company would probably turn around and sue you, which is why you need your contract to protect yourself. If all of this sounds intimidating, realize this example would be for when you are dealing with a very large company and handling sensitive data. If you work with smaller companies or do not handle sensitive data, you don't need quite as much. At a basic level, a mom-and-pop B2B customers might just want an official invoice, which is easy to create in the dashboard of your payment processor.

B2B customers generally want to use reliable products that are the best of the best. And they are willing to pay for that. You can charge more to businesses than you can to consumers, and you can charge large businesses more than small businesses. If you have worked at a company before, think of the products and services they used to help operate the business, and you will likely find this to be true.

B2B Validation

You are trying to reach individuals when validating your B2B ideas. You'll have to do a lot of cold calls, cold emails, cold tweets, cold LinkedIn connection requests, etc. When you reach out to your B2B prospect, you want to present your MVP, then follow up if you don't hear back. Most of the time, you won't get a reply, but you need only a few bites to validate your idea, and if you do enough outreach, eventually, a few people will respond. When they do, save their info for when the product is ready with all the bells and whistles included. If you continue to do outreach but aren't getting enough replies, your idea likely does not have demand within the industry, or you are not conveying your idea properly and/or completely.

Don't worry too much about perfecting your pitch for the MVP. You just need to find out if they like the idea you have presented. You're not selling anything. Your idea is doing the "selling" for you. All you need is to gauge interest.

Further Reading

B2B is super complex, but we have limited space to discuss the topic. I will leave you with one final thought: B2B is a continuum. At one end, you are selling to a mom-and-pop shop somewhere in the Midwest. At the other end, you are trying to speak with an international airline that operates in 58 countries. Most start by selling on the mom-and-pop end of the B2B continuum, then move towards the international airline end once adequate experienced is gained.

Two books I highly recommend to learn about B2B selling are *Selling to Big Companies* by Jill Konrath, and *Selling To The C-Suite* by Nicholas A.C. Read and Dr. Stephen Bistritz. If you explore further, you will find that there isn't a whole lot written about selling software to very large companies, which may be what you are looking for. For this topic, your best bet is consulting someone who has direct experience in purchasing software at that level. For me, I started talking to one of my clients named Greg who lives in Australia. He worked in IT management for 32 years before he quit to make money from search engine optimization. I let him pick my brain for juicy info on search engine optimization, and in return, he let me pick his brain for info related to selling software at the highest level. When you get stuck, actively seek out the information you need and keep your ears open. You can probably find someone who knows more about what you seek.

Business-to-Consumer

Your first software idea is probably a B2C software idea. Most entrepreneurs are fixated on the idea of selling to fellow consumers, which is fine. If you choose to take the B2C path, your focus will be on scaling your operation and making as many sales as possible with as little legwork from you as possible. Everything is automated. As an example, when you use Netflix, everything from the signup process to canceling your membership is done automatically. It has to be. As a B2C business, Netflix cannot afford to pay special attention to each customer like a business such as Oracle could.

You also need to think about customer service. You can't provide one-on-one service to every customer in a B2C relationship. You will quickly get overwhelmed. You must do everything possible to reduce interaction between yourself and the consumer. Things like FAQ sections and community forums can help. Study popular B2C websites and services and observe how they reduce customer interaction to see more.

You will need to be able to scale both your product and your customer support quickly if you wish to increase your B2C sales in a reliable way. Think of this task as a positive and not a negative. The scaling solutions might be tough to work out at the start, but once you are scalable, if you can find any success with a marketing campaign, you can simply dump more money into the campaign to earn more automatically. If you were doing B2B, this blunt and speedy scaling strategy would not work, as you would need to dedicate significant resources to each and every customer.

And, your expectations from B2C customers are far less than they are with B2B. A Netflix customer doesn't expect one-on-one support from the CEO, but a large B2B client might. That's just something to consider.

B2C Validation

There are a variety of ways to validate B2C ideas, because many people make consumer decisions, whereas few make decisions relevant to your B2B idea. You could post your MVP on forums. You could show it to random people you know. You could post it around Facebook and see if you get any interaction. Heck, you could even run a Kickstarter campaign and see if random consumers will give you money to build out your idea.

My favorite B2C validation method is using forums—in particular, Reddit. Reddit is the largest "forum" in existence today, with a category for almost any consumer interest imaginable. Gamers, equestrians, dog lovers, comedians, even weird sexual fetishes... you get the point. On Reddit, you can find any laser-targeted consumer group to show your MVP to.

I make a post on a relevant section of Reddit with my MVP, then see what happens. Does the post get "upvotes" (the equivalent of Likes on Facebook)? Do consumers comment on the post? You can get all of the feedback you need with a proper post. When you post, make sure you position yourself as a friend, doing others a favor, and just asking for honest feedback in return.

Don't come across as too "selly" or you may alienate Reddit consumers. Definitely don't mention that whatever you are talking about is your MVP for a business idea. They hate that.

If you make a post and Reddit loves it, you know you have something with potential. Reddit users are anonymous, and therefore brutally honest, so they will have no reluctance to share how they really feel. At the same time, if Reddit doesn't love your post, you will know exactly why, and you can use that feedback to educate yourself.

Further Reading

Unlike B2B, there are countless numbers of books covering B2C selling in general. One I would strongly recommend is *Growth Hacker Marketing: A Primer on the Future of PR, Marketing, and Advertising* by Ryan Holiday. Ryan gives you an inside look into how companies like Hotmail and Dropbox found their footing so quickly, and the information contained within is applicable to any B2C endeavour.

Ask Around the Industry

We talked about using industry forums and discussion boards to generate your idea, but you can use them again to validate your idea. Forums are true goldmines for aspiring entrepreneurs. Become a member of a relevant forum, post a thread with your MVP, and check if you are able to generate any interest. Prioritize forums with many members and lots of recent activity. (The first forum that pops up in Google might not be the best one to use.)

If people reply, you have the validation you need. If they don't, try to identify why you were unable to catch any interest. Did people view the thread, but not reply? That's a bad sign. Your idea might not be worthy, or you might just be using an inactive forum. Take forum validation seriously, but at the same time, don't get too discouraged until you try a few different forums, because each one might garner different results.

When you make your post on any forum, you want to pre-sell in a very mild way, and build interest around your name and/or brand name. Remember, you are not selling anything! Share a demo video, or screenshots, along with some explanatory info—and that's it. Don't even post your website URL unless someone asks, because that could come off as too promotional, and you might get banned.

Once you get some replies, you can reply to consumers to seek out advice that will aid you in the development of your product. You want to build your features based on user demand—that's what will make your product sell—so seeing what others need and want is of utmost importance. Do not ignore the thoughts of consumers! You may think you know best, but the consumer always knows best. You can also try replying to users on Reddit to determine consumer wants and needs, but forums tend to contain more invested members, meaning you have a much higher chance of developing fruitful back-and-forth conversations here.

Now, forums are slightly more difficult than Reddit in that the communities are tight-knit, meaning a brand new member posting a thread might not get any attention, regardless of the thread's merit. Even if it does get attention, that might not be the right attention—trolls are everywhere on forums (even business forums), and new members are trolled very frequently. Try to befriend a few forum members before you post the thread so you can popularize your thread and start the conversation off on the right foot. You can even ask your friends to sign up and participate on your thread to get things moving. If you opt to generate some feedback with any of these two methods, make sure the posts are unbiased and legitimate. You just want to get the conversation started so you can extract the genuine consumer input that you need to continue.

If you're a non-technical person and you want to create a startup or you want to create an app software extension, a bot, website, or whatever, the first thing you should do is get an advisor. Now, it doesn't have to be paid. You should just be like, "hey do you believe in this idea? Do you think I could do it?" Get feedback because a lot of times you'll build something that's not doable, technology-wise, no one's going to buy this or it already exists. There's a lot of conversations I have where I have to say, "hey, hey this already exists. You know like, oh really? Yeah, it's called Instagram." "No but we have filters"—"they do too." "Well we're going to have stories"—"ah dude I'll see you later." I'm serious. I judge a lot of hackathons, like just for the hell of it. And the amount of ideas that come out there. I'm like, I love your enthusiasm but that idea is already made, you know. I'll pull up a similar web or you know just random shit.

So, find an advisor, find someone you really admire in technology and if they don't want to spend time with you and they don't believe in the product that should be like the first hint, right. Ask 10 people.

DAVID MARKOVICH

FOUNDER, ONLINE GENIUSES

The Checklist

A couple years back, Entrepreneur released a fantastic outline of 20 questions that you should ask yourself when trying to validate your idea. Although the techniques and methods described within this book are more than enough to decide if your idea is worth pursuing, these 20 questions may help fill in any gaps.

1. What problem are you solving?
2. How have others attempted to solve this problem before, and why did their solutions succeed or fail?
3. How many specific benefits for your product or idea can you list?
4. Can you state, in clear language, the key features of your product or service?
5. Does your idea already exist in the same way you were going to create it?
6. Who are your potential competitors?
7. What key features does my product or service have that others will have a hard time copying?
8. Have you done a SWOT analysis?
9. Do you have access to the various resources you need to launch a business?

10. Do you have a mentor or industry advisor that you can call on?
11. Can you name somebody who would benefit from your product or service?
12. What is the size of the market that will buy your product or service?
13. Have you reached out to potential customers for feedback?
14. Can you set up a landing page and encourage interested people to sign up for more information?
15. What would it take to build a minimum viable product to test the market?
16. Can you get paying customers from your target market to pre-order based on a blueprint or mockup?
17. Can you produce the actual product yourself, or do you have a partner who can?
18. Do you have distributors or partners to help you scale your business?
19. What will it take to break even or make a profit?
20. How can investors in your idea make a profit?

The problem with startup ideas is that they all sound bad. E.g., Google was the 13th search engine and its algorithm didn't use metatags. Facebook was the 3rd social network and was only for Ivy League colleges. AirBnB was a platform website where you could find a stranger's house to sleep in (somebody's gonna get murdered). Lyft and Uber were (and still are) outright illegal in most cities. Good startup ideas sound like bad startup ideas. The problem is that bad startup ideas also sound like bad startup ideas.

PETER HUDSON
FOUNDER, SHELFIE

THE FOUNDATION OF YOUR MVP

Websites / Landing Pages

We just talked about MVPs. The concept of developing a MVP might have overwhelmed you. Don't worry! In the earliest stages of your product, even a MVP isn't a requirement. Instead, you can just pretend the software exists, and that it is every bit as incredible as you say. If you do that, you can still get feedback, without spending time or money on actual development. We're going to develop a website (likely just a single page) for starters. Your website will contain text, images, a call-to-action, and maybe an explanatory video. This type of website is called a landing page. New prospects arrive here, learn about your product, and decide whether they want it or not.

Building Landing Pages Immediately

A friend of mine, Noah, works on all sorts of products, from weight loss pills all the way to pillowcases. One day, we were trying to validate an idea that had to do with a unified cloud email inbox, and when I asked him how we should do it, he said, "set up a landing page within the very first hour."

When you first get an idea, you will feel a burst of energy, excitement, and restlessness flow through your veins to the very core of your body. Use this energy to write out what your product is about and attempt to sell it. This process helps you use your massive stores of energy to get a broad outline for the project, and any notes you make may become invaluable at a later point when you find yourself needing to hire development talent or sway investors to your corner.

I think it's important to get the landing page built right away, and there's actually a word for this it's called vaporware. It's essentially the process of creating advertising for something that doesn't exist in order to measure the popularity of it. Kickstarter is a good example of something that works in this zone, where not only is it a good way to raise money if it works but also a good barometer if people give a crap. I do recommend that people do this in the early stages of thinking about a product since it's much easier to make a little video or an ad or a landing page about what you think you want to create than it is to actually create the thing you wanna create then that is where you can start getting validation. You can see click through rates, you can see sign up rates, you can see reactions, you can see people sharing it and that's something that's big. Sometimes it's a little trickier than usual. For example, say it's a piece of hardware that you're talking about. You're going to somehow need to have mockups of it. If it's software you're gonna need to have screenshots. You've gotta have something for people to look at. There's times it's not so cut and dry you're going to have to put a little bit of effort in but it's certainly easier than taking it right to production.

ILAN NASS

FOUNDER, TAKTICAL DIGITAL

How to Build Your Landing Page

Once you decide to build your landing page, also called a squeeze page, the first decision you need to make is whether you will design it from scratch, or use a landing page builder service. Designing from scratch certainly has its benefits—it's cheaper, and you have more flexibility. But landing page builders are much faster, and, if you're a beginner, you likely do not have the design skill needed to match the quality of the pages you can build with a service. In general, using a landing page builder is good to get something functional up fast, and you can hire a designer to build you a custom, higher-converting landing page later.

Two popular landing page builders are Unbounce and LeadPages. Many of my industry friends use these two services to get their websites up and running. I personally make them myself, as I am more frugal and I know how to design. Choose the option that is best for you. You can always switch things up if you find that a from-scratch landing page is too difficult, or a builder landing page is too simplistic.

Unbounce is a pretty good option when it comes to landing pages. So what Unbounce does is that it lets you put together a website or a webpage just by dragging and dropping the interface, no code necessary. That's one way. If you want something a little bit more in depth there's these ready-to-build ready-to-go back ends such as Wordpress, Wix, and Squarespace. A lot of people use that as like an early way to get started before they have to build something that's more customized. LeadPages is popular as well. I've never used it but I hear a lot of good things. There's plenty of tools out there that allow you to throw together a landing page. Even Wordpress has a landing page that you can jump onto. So it's really not that hard. There's even Instapage, along with a few others. There shouldn't be a problem creating a landing page, even if you have no technical experience it can be done.

ILAN NASS

FOUNDER, TAKTICAL DIGITAL

Somewhere along the line, you will want to learn how to build your own websites. Basic website building is a key skill that all online entrepreneurs need to have a basic grasp of.

Building It Quick

Luckily, building a website is pretty easy. You need only two things: a domain name, and website hosting. In general, domain names are around $10-15 per year, and website hosting is $5-10 per month. You can buy the domain and hosting from the same company, or you can buy them separately. Buying separately is usually cheaper and more flexible.

Your domain name is like your website's physical address. When people type in your domain, they go to your website. But by itself, a domain name isn't anything. You need to have something at your physical address for people to see. Your web hosting files are the meat of your website. A visitor types in your domain name and goes to your website, where your website files load to present the website to the visitor.

I use InternetBS, Namecheap, and Name.com to buy my domains. These three domain registrars are solid and buying a domain is very cut-and-dry. Hosting companies are a little different. They change every couple of years to every couple of months. So instead of recommending a particular company that may be unreliable by the time you read this book, I will recommend that you do some basic research to find the best current options.

As a beginner, you should understand that web hosting is incredibly complex overall... but not for you. You just need something basic. Look for Linux hosting with cPanel. cPanel is a web server interface that makes your life a whole lot easier. You'll see options for shared hosting, VPS hosting, and dedicated hosting. You can usually started with shared hosting, as it is the cheapest.

Once you buy your hosting, you will receive nameservers in the introductory email. Nameservers connect your domain to your hosting. Go to your domain registrar's dashboard and set your nameservers to the records you just received. If you get confused, you can look up how to set your nameservers, and your hosting company will likely have a step-by-step tutorial. Once you set your nameservers, you have your domain, and you have the ability to put a website on that domain through your hosting.

Check the introductory email again and use the cPanel information to log into your cPanel dashboard. Now we are going to install WordPress. WordPress is an easy-to-use and very popular content management system. You can create landing pages, and even more complex websites, without writing a single line of code. To install WordPress, look for Softalacous in your cPanel dashboard and follow the instructions. If Softalacous is not available, go to WordPress.org and follow the instructions there.

If the above sounds confusing to you, you may be better off using a landing page builder, as you just sign up and use the drag-and-drop interface to create your page, instead of dealing with all of the technical aspects.

Parts of a Landing Page

The goal of your landing page is to explain what your product is to a random person in an easy-to-understand way. Your landing page does not have to be particularly lengthy! In fact, that can detract from your ability to explain your product concisely. Visitors will get bored, especially if you do a poor job explaining.

You really only need a few different elements in your MVP landing page. To start, you need a USP (unique selling proposition). Your USP is usually just your headline and sub-headline. Your visitors don't care too much about your product, so you have to grab their interest quick. After your USP, you put a video or image with some explanatory text, which allows the visitor to learn more about your product after you have caught their interest. Finally, you lead the user from interest to action with a call-to-action, which prompts the user to do something that you want him to do. On your MVP landing page, your call-to-action should be an email box with a submit button. When the user inputs his email and clicks submit, his information is added to your email list, which is a valuable tool for getting sales further down the line. You can use an email subscription platform like Aweber to collect these leads without technical knowledge. I recommend Aweber because according to a study done by a well-known marketer named Jeremy Schoemaker, they have the best email delivery rates. (You don't want to send emails to the spam box.)

A landing page is all you really need to communicate what you do. You got to work on your value prop. You need a headline and subtitle to explain what you do.

You can show someone a landing page for 5 seconds, either online or a piece of paper. Then you hide it and ask them a couple questions such as, "what do you think this product was?" or "does it appear trustworthy?" and you can spot if you have clarity problems. That is a really rapid way to try to improve the communication of your value prop, which is super important.

These can be people on the street or your friends. Ideally, you want people who don't understand what you do, because if you can communicate with people who don't then you're really getting the clarity nail. I would do a mix of people who understand that space and those who don't. After finding your target customer, try to find people in their network. You have to test it with a broad spectrum of people. Research and insights are the key and if you do that from day 1, you'll be ahead of most people.

OLI GARDNER

CO-FOUNDER, UNBOUNCE

How to Think of a Brand Name

Now you know how to get your website up and running. But first, you need to decide on a domain name for your product. Here are a few ways you can come up with a name both you and your customers will love.

Descriptive Phrase

I like to use a simple method of naming my products: I name them based on usage. Keyword Scout is a keyword research tool; you know what it is even if you just know its name. My other projects follow the same lines of thinking. SerpClix is a click-exchange network used to help increase Google rankings. Shout Our Biz is a social media marketplace for businesses. SEO Expositor generates and analyzes search engine optimization reports. You get the picture.

When using this type of name generation idea, my main weapon of choice is the thesaurus. I came up with Keyword Scout by plugging "research" into the thesaurus. One of the synonyms for "research" was "scout." Simple as that.

One Word

Apple, Instagram, and Twitter all make no sense when you hear them without context. If you had never heard of Apple, you would think that the company has something to do with the fruit. But today, when you hear "apple," you immediately think of the technology company, unless the context draws you to think of the fruit specifically. In general, one-word names are highly brandable, with the cost of the product not being instantly understandable when the company first forms.

> *The name actually came from a shortened, fun version of "Demonstration"—I just thought of it while on a plane ride. Loved the name, so I ended up buying it from the owner (Demio.com) for $10,000. We actually got the domain dem.io afterwards as a gift.*
>
> **WYATT JOZWOWSKI**
> *CO-FOUNDER, DEMIO*

> *Rick had a placeholder domain which was called ezlanding.com which I thought was just absolutely appalling and everybody agreed. He just got*

it because it was available. I'm a big branding geek so I was hell bent on figuring out a name that was better than that. I was out walking one night and I said, "well what's bad about marketing? Well lots of things. Bounce rate is bad, and how do you reverse that, well you can 'un' it." I actually sprinted home because I couldn't find the domain in my phone for some reason so I sprinted home at like 1 AM to buy it. Like someone was going to buy it, other than me, at 1 AM.

Then I had to convince the team. I was with Justin, and we got really drunk and we put "un" in front of it, so he was on board. Then it took a couple weeks for the rest to come on board, then everything we did after that, I made sure I came up with the name for it.

OLI GARDNER

CO-FOUNDER, UNBOUNCE

Translation

Translations can give you brandable names without the arduous task of finding a nice one-word name that has not been used already. Explain your product in two or three words, then pop those words into an online translator. Go through each language translation (French, Spanish, etc.) and read the pronunciations aloud as an English speaker would. Wait until you find a word, or a combination of words, that look and sound good to you. You will eventually find something you love, and that name will be highly unique.

Credo is actually the second brand name that I've operated under. So, I started the business that's called HireGun. I bought HireGun.co and launched under that. Basically, a play off the term gun for hire. I started to work for myself end of September, early October 2013 and kind of launched out the gate in November. So, there were a couple of things going on at that time. It was all the hullabaloo in the US about gun control and a lot of that stuff going on and so I started to feel a little uneasy about it and then I was thinking should I rebrand or not. It was going to be a lot of work. Then the pushing factor was when I flew across the country from San Francisco to

Virginia where my parents lived and landed off that flight, it was the day before Thanksgiving, I had emails from a lawyer in New York City saying that I was infringing upon his client's trademark. It was an agency in New York called The Hired Guns and they did have the trademark and I was infringing on it, you know, completely naively, I wasn't trying to do it. They basically gave me 2½ months, well I negotiated 2½ months to rebrand. It took me about two months. The hardest part was finding the name; finding a name that wasn't already trademarked and you know, meant something. So basically, Credo is a play on, Italian for belief. I like to think that Credo is a values-driven company. It connotes trust. And there's credibility to all the people on the platform because I personally vet all of them. I talk to them on the phone, I see their clients before they're even allowed to pay me to be on the platform.

JOHN DOHERTY
FOUNDER, CREDO

We did a lot of research having named previous startups really badly and so we did a lot of research into what the requirements were and having read quite a lot of interesting articles about what makes a successful name we realized we wanted something catchy, memorable and something that kind of evoked let's say some kind of either emotion or sensory kind of aspect so that again it becomes more memorable. We knew the heat map was going to be one of the most important features so were looking for a name that had like all of the senses we knew; heat like temperature would be a good one. So after failing to find names that were available. We resorted to going looking at premium domain sites because they've pretty much registered every name there is. Although we were bootstrapped we did put some money into the company and we thought this would be a great way to use some money. We looked at premium domains and we spent hours going through them all and I'll never forget the moment we found Hotjar, because the fact that we were doing all in one, bringing multiple tools together. We loved the idea of the jar and we could quickly visualize how we could explain that and how easy it would be for other people to remember the name.

DR. DAVID DARMANIN

CO-FOUNDER, HOTJAR

You don't have to obsess over your name, as you can always change it later. But names of companies do matter. The general rule of startups in tech is you stick with two syllables. Either stick to something that describes your product to some degree or you can go with a nonsensical word like Google or Twitter. But you'll notice that a lot of these guys stick with the 2 syllable rule and they stick with simple. They try not to get overly complex with their logos. There logos are either word marks or very simple shapes. And flat design kind of thing. A name and a brand is nice to have. I wouldn't necessarily stop my testing because I couldn't come up with a good name. And that's the thing you can ask friends and family for advice on.

…and I don't recommend anybody misspell a word as their company name. Taktical is spelt with a K and it's the worst idea I've ever had because you're constantly explaining to people that no it's not spelled like that. It's T-A-K-T-I-C-A-L, and they're like wait, tack… no tak. I've had so many cases of people misspelling the company name, it's outrageous. That was kind of a weird moment. There was a company at the time that was popular called Mekanism. Mekanism was a creative agency, they were doing a lot of ads for red bull and I thought their name was really cool and they had a "K" in their name. And Taktical, the name Taktical came to me because I found that so many agencies were strategic in nature. They're all like, we do strategic planning for your marketing. And I'm like that's great, strategy is great but who's going to implement the strategy? You've gotta get tactical at some point, you've gotta get down in the dirt, get your hands dirty, go through the data and make micro decisions on a daily basis. Who does that? And that's when I decided to name the company Taktical. And that's kind

of the way to juxtapose ourselves against everyone else in the space and I also took the K out from the word marketing. The original design was supposed to be for Taktical Marketing where the K would cross then I ditched the marketing part. And the rest stuck, and it kind of took off from there. When you've got a brand name and a reputation in New York City, it's kind of too late to change it.

ILAN NASS

FOUNDER, TAKTICAL DIGITAL

Expensive Dot Com

You may look around and find that other people have already snatched up all of the perfect domain names you had in mind. Whoever owns the domain will probably ask you for a high fee in exchange for it: thousands of dollars, or more.

Sanjay Singhal, the founder of Audiobooks.com, was one of the people who purchased a high-ticket domain for his brand name. When asked about the domain name purchase in an interview, he replied, "$850,000... best deal I ever made."

You may be able to buy a high-ticket domain name and see success. But this approach is not feasible for most people. We're still in the validation phase of our project. Spending a fortune on something like a domain name isn't the best use of your funds. If you have your heart set on having an amazing domain name, start first with one of the other methods of domain name generation beforehand, then purchase your ideal name once you know beyond a doubt that the project has potential.

Pretending to Sell

You have your name. You know how to make your website. We have discussed what you should put on your website (USP, more details, and a call-to-action). Great! But you still might be confused on what to put on your website in regards to the USP and the details you include.

Your mindset should be that you are selling your product. Pretend your product is made and you are doing everything you can to convince the visitor of its merit so that he will take the leap and make a purchase. If you employ this strategy, once you reach the call-to-action section of your page, you will have done everything possible to get the visitor interested enough to purchase.

Just one difference: you aren't asking for a purchase in your call-to-action. You are asking for an email submission. By asking for an email submission, you are able to gauge sales interest even without a product to sell. If someone is interested, he will enter his email instead of just leaving the page. This email submission rate can be enormously insightful when validating your product.

Email submissions also allow you to build a list of hyper-interested potential buyers. Consider this list to be worth its weight in gold! 100 red-hot email subscribers might earn you more than 3,000 cold visitors would. A friend of mine, Joshua Zamora, once told me about how he revealed to his wife how much a single email blast could earn him. The very next day, his wife came home with a brand new decked-out refrigerator, and left a note saying, "it was expensive, but only half of an email blast!" Marketers with massive lists can earn a normal full-year salary with a single blast.

Driving Traffic

You're finally ready to start sending traffic to your landing page. By itself, your landing page is nothing. No one cares. You need to bring in traffic so users can interact with the landing page and you can judge the validity of your idea.

I wouldn't start with Facebook ads right away. You could, but you know, Facebook costs money and so usually what I would do is if I had a product and I had identified a group of people that might be interested in that product I might try finding where they live on the internet. If it's Reddit or a forum or some sort of a chat. A lot of tech people like to use Product Hunt now as a place to launch things. And so you could just find these things and post your offering in these places and see if it gets attention. That's the first step I would take just to see if anybody bites. Now, that's a tall order because you might get lost in the shuffle of a lot of things going on in that forum or maybe these people are just not collecting anywhere very much and you can't find them so the alternative is then to do Facebook or Google ads. And

Google ads are more appropriate if this is your product or your solution is the kind of thing people are searching for. And you just built a better one or you know people are looking for it. Facebook ads are better if you think people would never know about this product if it was never shown to them. The problem with Facebook ads is that you have this extra layer of variables which is the advertisement itself, so as if it's not bad enough that you have to kind of find out if your product is any good or your landing page is any good or your targeting is correct, but now you get the added problem of having to kind of write a good Facebook ad. In and of itself, you can spend weeks optimizing just the ad before you optimize anything else. So it does create a bit of a layer there. I also think that it doesn't give you as good of feedback as if you tried to get into a community. LinkedIn groups, Facebook groups, whatever if you get to work your way into a community of people and kind of test the waters there you can get feedback. People will talk to you, they'd respond to you, that doesn't happen on Facebook very much. Sometimes ads can get shares and stuff but it's very rare that people will outright tell you, "well this is the problem that I see with your product" unless you ask for it. Should you be collecting emails? Absolutely. There is no doubt. Like, if you're not collecting emails on your landing pages, what are you doing?

ILAN NASS

FOUNDER, TAKTICAL DIGITAL

Pay-Per-Click Advertising

The vast majority of internet advertising falls into the PPC (pay-per-click) category, where an advertiser pays the advertising network for every click on an ad. If Bauer Hockey wanted to advertise on ESPN, the company would submit its ad, get it live on the ESPN platform, and pay a certain amount every time an ESPN visitor made the leap from ESPN to Bauer's landing page. If every click costs $2.00, then the cost-per-click (CPC) is $2.00. There are a variety of ways to bid for clicks, such as CPM, where you pay for every 1,000 times your ad is served instead of every time it is clicked on, but everything ultimately boils down to how much you pay for a click. CPCs vary based on the advertising network you use and the industry you are targeting. In general, the most profitable the industry, the higher the CPC will be. Targeting people who want to lose weight will result in a high CPC; targeting people who play video games will results in low CPC.

The two dominant PPC advertising networks are Adwords and Facebook. Between these two networks, you can target virtually any audience you are trying to reach. There are also other types of networks, such as native advertising networks, but for our purposes, we will focus on just Google and Facebook, as you generally need significant experience in advertising with PPC to get any value from anything else.

On Google, you can place your ads above the search results for almost any keyword search, and on Facebook, you can show your ad to anyone who matches a certain set of interest or behavioral criteria. The advertising network you should use depends on who you are trying to reach. If you are trying to reach 50-year-old businessmen, you might have trouble targeting them on Facebook, but Google will work just fine. On the other hand, if you are trying to reach 23-year-olds with an Xbox, advertising might be difficult and expensive on Google, but easy and cheap on Facebook.

Both networks rely on the same type of ad format. You get a few lines of text to get the user interested enough to click your ad. On Facebook, you also get a picture to help you out. You need to write a good ad to ensure that you get clicks—merely creating an ad does not guarantee you will get anyone interested.

Write your ad and get someone on Fiverr to design an attractive picture to complement it if you are using Facebook. Then submit your ad. Spend $50 or $100 on traffic. See what happens. Maybe you get a good number of clicks and you are able to validate your idea, either positively or negatively. If you don't get any clicks, or your CPC is outrageously high, do not despair! You might have a good idea, but not the advertising skills necessary to present it through a paid advertising network. PPC can be an excellent advertising strategy for any online business, but you do need to use the platforms with skill to achieve the results you desire.

In the case of Shelfie, we used SurveyMonkey's "buy audience" feature and got 1000 people we didn't know to answer a 15 question survey about how much they'd be willing to pay for a digital version of a book they already owned in print.

PETER HUDSON

FOUNDER, SHELFIE

Personal Social Media Accounts

Directly asking friends and family for idea validation can leave you with dishonest feedback, as we discussed earlier. But chances are, if you have any active social media profiles, not everyone on there is closely related to you. Thus, they are more likely to provide accurate feedback. And, if you make your post public and any one of your social friends shares it to other people, your potential for good feedback multiplies.

Social media users love videos. Adding a video to your post on your personal social media accounts will boost your chances of success by quite a bit. If you have money to spend ($50 or more), you can head to Upwork.com and find a qualified video freelancer to make a custom video for you. If you don't have much of a budget ($50 or less), you can head over to Fiverr and get a templated video made for just a couple of bucks. Templated videos aren't quite as good as custom videos are, but adding any sort of video whatsoever will help.

You will need to write a video script to give to your designer. So what should you include in your video? You can combine your video animation with an audio track to convey an enormous amount of information in a short span of time. There are countless resources available on this topic, which you should can consult beforehand to make sure your video is as good as it can be, even on a small budget. Below is the script I used for SerpClix, which may provide valuable insight into the structure and flow of a promotional video.

Voice	Animation
SerpClix is a SERP (pronounced serp) click exchange network used to rank websites higher by increasing the click-through rate for your website, for a given keyword.	Flash logo
	Show screen of a computer searching keyword, scrolling through down Google results to click a specific website on the Google search results.
You see, we bridge the connection between website owners and clickers.	Show a group of webmasters and a group of workers
You, the website owner, provide a desired keyword and URL.	Show a person speaking these: Keyword: Toronto chiropractor URL: www.GindeleFamilyChiropractic.com
We calculate the required searches that the keyword will need to increase ranking.	Show calculations and groups of mouse cursors.
We distribute the task to thousands of people and incentivize them to search your keyword phrase and visit your website.	Show coins being divided up to clickers (people). Ideally there are hundreds of clickers.
Each clicker searches your keyword and clicks to your website.	Show screen of a computer searching keyword, scrolling through down Google results to click a specific website on the Google search results.

All clickers are tracked and managed through our browser extension to ensure maximum quality.	Show a user navigating the random website they landed on. Clicking around, scrolling down, clicking.
That means no bots, only the highest quality of real human visitors to your website.	X through a picture of a robot, and show some real people waving.
Sign up for SerpClix today to start ranking.	Show an arrow going upward on a graph to simulate rank increases. Then the company logo. Basically, show desired results!

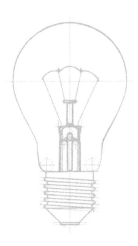

CHAPTER 3

• • • • • • • •

IS IT A FIT FOR YOU?

Now you have validated your idea, and you have determined that it is indeed a good idea! The next step is determining whether the product is something that you, yourself, should make. Not every good idea is one that you should pursue.

The truth is that good ideas are in abundance. You can probably validate five different ideas in a short amount of time if you set your mind to it. But following through on a project takes much more work than simply conceptualizing and validating a project does. You don't want to pursue just any valid idea. You want to pursue one that meshes well with your current skillset, experience, and more. The following questions will allow you to make a determination as to whether your valid idea is worth pursuing *for you.*

I think that every idea is different in that there's some ideas that don't require connections or understanding or depth of understanding. Where some ideas might be totally unique that they don't exist. Snapchat is an example of like there's no specific place where that idea would be tested. It's kind of a solution to a broad issue, whereas for example, I have a real estate project and it's kind of an Airbnb offshoot and the reason we're able to make profit off it because I know people in New York City real estate. I know a lot of brokers. My partner in the deal is a guy who is deeply embedded in the real estate community, he knows all the developers, he knows all the processes, he knows how the industry works so he's able to leverage a lot of that knowledge and those connections. Whereas someone with this same exact product may not be able to do that if they don't have those connections. And so that plays a very large role I think. But it doesn't play a very large role all the time. When you're looking at a particular idea you kind of have to consider this. Are there federal regulations in your space? If you're, for example, using an investment crowdfunding platform like Kickstarter, it has regulation issues to worry about or Uber, they had to know how drivers and taxi cabs worked. The logistics of it all. Are you trying to sell to enterprise companies as clients, and are you connected with those people? It's very tough, very tough. And very much so the people who figure out the connections are the ones that are able to catapult the company that may not even be as good as someone else's product but they were able to take steps faster because of those connections. So yeah, I think that matters a lot. More than people might realize. If you're trying to sell to bars or restaurants and you don't know any restauranteurs and you don't know the industry, you're going to have a hard time getting through the door. So yeah, I think that's a big deal. But not every product has that. Some products don't have that issue at all because they're not associated or there's no string attaching them to any particular sector of the economy.

ILAN NASS

FOUNDER, TAKTICAL DIGITAL

Does the Revenue Potential Match Your Financial Goals?

You might have other motivations for developing your software aside from profits. But you cannot ignore the financial aspect of an idea. If you build out an idea only to find that it does not earn you enough to justify the work put in, you will get burned out and discouraged.

Think of what financial milestone you hope to achieve if you build out and sell your product successfully. Maybe you're a student and you need only a couple hundred dollars per month to be living large. Maybe you're happy with your life but struggling financially, and you need only a couple thousand to cover rent and living expenses. Or maybe you have your sights set high, and you want to make enough to buy two houses on the beach, 10 exotic cars, and a life of pure luxury each and every day you wake up. No matter what you desire, understanding that desire and ensuring your idea can meet that desire is 100% necessary.

> *My brother once did a big study on successful entrepreneurs and (because there's a lot of stories about someone being 12 and successful) and there are guys who started a company at the age of 60 and are successful, but those really are the outliers. If you plot the starting age of the founder versus success, you get a bell curve with a maximum around the age of 37-38.*
>
> **FRANK VAN MIERLO**
> *FOUNDER, 1366 TECHNOLOGIES*

Now it's time to "be realistic." If you just imagined that you want to make a few billion dollars with one of your first projects, you need to take a second to think about that. You are just starting. This is your first project, or one of your first. You probably do not have the current experience and skillset to create a product worth billions. And you probably can't dedicate nearly enough time and effort to it if you have to work a job on the side; that's for sure. If you begin by trying to make billion-dollar products, you will very likely fail at every single idea, and become very discouraged. Failure is an excellent teacher, but when you do nothing but fail, failure becomes a negative.

Balance your mental resources with your financial goals. If you have to work to cover living expenses, start by trying to cover living expenses and have some extra money on the side so that you can pursue your lofty goals properly. No matter what level you are at, aim to succeed within that level, but do not attempt to jump to the top, because if it were that easy, everyone would be doing it.

I know it sounds it sounds kind of a little bit materialistic but in the end what are you looking to achieve? I ask this to many entrepreneurs that I advise or mentor. Which is the first question, what are you trying to achieve? Do you want to just work from home and be relaxed? Or do you want to buy a Lamborghini? Do you know what I mean? As in not that a Lamborghini would be the most inspiring thing to have but some people think that way so it's good to recognize that because if you do want to buy a Lamborghini you can't start with like a tiny idea that can't scale. So, it's good to start from that position. Or the third example, are you passionate about an idea, do you want to change the world? So that's another way of thinking about it.

DR. DAVID DARMANIN

CO-FOUNDER, HOTJAR

Does the Idea Interest You?

When you think of a new idea, you are excited. You think about it all the time! Maybe you can't sleep because of how excited you are. You think your motivation at the start will never wear off…

Your motivation will, in fact, wear off. Building and planning a software idea is not always particularly interesting exciting or interesting. You will go through "dry phases" when your interest is lowered, such as when you are tackling a big technical problem that is preventing you from moving forward. As an example, imagine you are single and you just met someone new. For the first month or two, everything is perfect no matter what, and you don't consider breaking it off, because everything is perfect. But as time goes on, all the little things start to add up, and you have to consider if the relationship is even worth it. Maybe you break it off, or maybe you stick with it because you can truly see how it would work in the end. Your development efforts are the exact same. You are currently in the honeymoon phase of your idea. Once you have been working on it for a while, will you feel the same as you do now?

There is no surefire way to determine if you will be able to maintain motivation throughout the duration of developing an idea, just as there is no surefire way to guarantee that a new relationship will work out, but I will give you some insight into my personal thought process when it comes to ideas

(I'll leave the dating advice for someone else). When I come up with a valid new idea, I have some restless nights, and you will, too. But that's normal. If I *continue* to think about the idea and work on it for *two full weeks* without losing motivation, I determine the idea has passed the test. This strategy is not perfect, but I have found it to work pretty well.

> *In my opinion, 8 out of 10 projects have zero chance of success. It is an optimistic assumption, I should say.*
>
> **SASHA ANDRIEIEV**
> *CEO, JELVIX*

Is the Industry Reasonable?

Maybe you like cell phones and you think you can compete with cellular providers to provide a better service. The cell service industry is one that is not reasonable for a beginner. The barrier of entry is absolutely enormous. Even at this point in my life, with a number of successful projects under my belt, I would not have the slightest clue as to where to start, aside from hiring a lawyer who knows the laws and regulations that protect those wireless cartels.

Many industries are like this. The good news is that the barrier to entry in the software industry is very low comparatively. Anybody can become somebody with a successful piece of software. You develop it and sell it. If you can do that, you're in.

The exception to this point is if you are developing software for one of those tricky industries. Imagine you are a school teacher, and your first thought is to sell educational software. Well, you are going to be pitching your idea to a small group of buyers who control what software is used in which school district. Behind their buying decisions will be a myriad of considerations, regulations, and politics that you are simply unaware of. Your experience as a teacher may not be enough to break into an industry like education as a software seller. However, experience can go far in some cases—kids know social media better than most others, for example.

There are other factors at play besides pure experience. Consider the size of the industry. I did six figures with Keyword Scout because I went into an industry that was relatively niche. That decision was good because it was easier to enter into and I saw success. But I was also limited in the number of copies of software I could sell. Perhaps if I picked something different I could have done seven figures instead of just six. Who knows? The point is that although many industries can be entered, not all of those industries will have the same level of difficulty or revenue potential.

[When deciding whether or not to invest,] we look at both, [the team and the idea], but focus on the founders. Think of a ship crossing the ocean that just left port. It seems like it's pointed in a good direction. Since they'll have to make many adjustments along the way, we want to make sure the ship has a good captain as well.

DANIEL GROSS

PARTNER, Y COMBINATOR

What Are Your Chances of Success?

I've considered starting a social network, as many other entrepreneurs have. Successful social networks have the potential to grow at a rapid pace. The problem is that successful social networks are *so* rare. You've heard of Facebook. You've heard of Instagram. But have you heard of the tens of thousands of social networks that never got off the ground?

I'm not doubting you, and I'm not doubting myself, either. There are just better options for you to pursue. Usually, I execute ideas that are related to an industry I know at least somewhat well. Maybe I have worked within in it before, or I have friends who have. I don't just latch onto any idea that sounds good on paper. Don't let fear of failure hold you back, but always consider your chances of success, too.

What Do You Have to Lose?

Bear with me for a moment while I sound like your parents. Where are you in life? Student? Working? Young enough that your parents can support you if you fail? Old enough that your family will suffer if you fail?

If you're a student, you could throw caution to the wind put all of your time and money into an idea. If you're single and working, you could still take a big risk and invest all of your spare time and money into an idea—but not everything, because then you would crash and burn in a serious way if you fail. If you're working and supporting a family, you could pursue projects that require minimal time investment to adapt around your busy life and ensure your family does not suffer. You have a certain amount of time and money you can realistically commit to an idea, and you would be wise to pursue projects that match this level of commitment.

Do You Have Any Personal Advantages?

What is your unfair advantage over the competition? Let's say I am in direct competition with you. This situation is not unrealistic; you will be entering into a market and probably competing with other software owners who are businessmen. What is the ace up your sleeve? If you have an advantage that others do not have, that can be your ticket to success.

Despite what you may have heard, you do want to surround yourself with a small barrier of entry to prevent just anyone from doing what you do. If anyone can do it, you might struggle. Can't think of a direct advantage? Consider the people you know. You might not know a single individual who could be considered a true "business connection," but your friends, family, and even coworkers can all be tapped to give you an upper hand.

How Quickly Can You Bring Your Idea to Market?

My experience has taught me that faster is better. If you can bring a software to market fast, you can determine quickly whether the idea is worth your time or not, and you prevent yourself from wasting time and money on hypothetically valid ideas that turn out to be duds.

When I was 15, I taught myself basic coding, and made simple software that could be coded one night, then sold or monetized the very next day. These days, I work on bigger ideas, and developing a MVP might take more than a single day. Someone like Elon Musk might work on much loftier projects, with his time to execute and validate an idea being much longer than where I am currently at. When you start, you're better off acting like I did at 15 over how Elon Musk acts today.

Determining how quickly I can bring a product to market is actually one of my largest influencing factors when deciding on a project. I make a list of ideas, validate them, and then choose which one to pursue based on which idea can be executed in the shortest amount of time. Getting your product into the marketplace is very important. I can't stress this enough.

PART 2

• • • • • • • •

The Development Stage

The basis of this book is the idea that you do not have to be a programmer in order to be the owner of a software company. Now that you have your idea ready to go, we are ready to get started with exactly that. You do not have to know how to code in order to succeed! In fact, although I do know a few programming languages, my most successful projects have always been made by others.

So the first year I just worked by myself and I paid for everything, which was an easy thing to do because my first venture was tremendously successful and a lot of people made a lot of money at the end of that. Even my previous venture Bluefin, I started working 2 years with no pay. My story has always been, at the beginning of the venture, you just work for free. At some point you start paying people, but first you put together the team. I had the team of 10 people, who were willing to join but hadn't joined yet. The only person working full time on the venture was me but the other people were waiting in the wings saying, "as soon as you have money, we will quit our jobs and join" and then we raised around $12 million and then almost everybody joined, except one guy who said he was going to join but willfully did not join. Then we got started.

FRANK VAN MIERLO

FOUNDER, 1366 TECHNOLOGIES

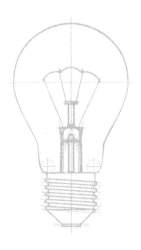

CHAPTER 4

• • • • • • • •

Partners? Staff?

The world of software development can easily fit into two categories with very little exception in between. You have your traditional "startups"—basically, what you think of when you think of the word *startup*. These entrepreneurs work in a techy place like Silicon Valley, raise massive investment to fund their ideas (often before they have made a single cent), and in turn, receive massive valuations if successful. That's one way to do things.

Then, there is the other group of software developers. These people do not work in Silicon Valley. You've probably never heard of them. They work anywhere in the world. They outsource their programming needs to remote teams of workers located all around the world. They don't necessarily change the world or receive millions in investment funding, but they do provide useful solutions, and they do get to keep every penny they earn. They are free to do what they want, and they earn very handsomely when they succeed.

Both ways are valid paths to success as a software company owner. Silicon Valley is filled with ragtag founders finding success and millions.

Think Uber, PayPal, and Snapchat. The second group has plenty of successes, too, though you might not hear about them, because they are not in the news unless you're looking. Companies like Demio, Market Hero, and JvZoo were started by people in the second group of software developers, and despite starting without massive investment, they still earned their founders millions in a very short time. There are countless other examples, just like that, in both groups. We will cover both groups, with a heavy emphasis on the second group (the self-starters), as that's what I know best, and likely the group you will be in if you act on what you read in this book.

Partners

The one-man-army can work fantastically well in many situations, but statistically in the startup world, single founders are rare. Y Combinator is a well-known seed accelerator, which means they give a relatively small investment, but access to many useful services, in exchange for some equity in a company. The very few projects they do decide to back are mostly made up of teams of at least two people. Investors aren't dumb, and the fact that they usually pick teams of two or more should not be ignored.

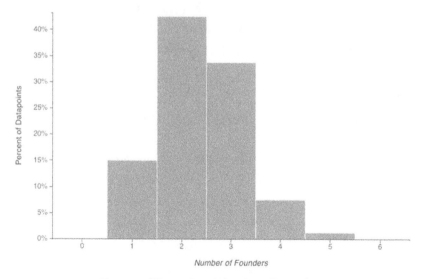

Percent of Datapoints / Number of Founders

Personally, I have always been a solopreneur despite knowing these statistics, but doing so has its costs. You have more freedom, but teams are generally more motivated. Teams also have much wider skillsets. And due to the fact that multiple people are working on one project, teams can get things done much faster.

We prefer cofounders, two or three. Ideally one technical, one non-technical. It's psychologically easier when you have a cofounder. But that's far from being a rule so I'd say something like a quarter to a third of our founders are solo.

SANJAY SINGHAL

CANADIAN VENTURE PARTNER, 500 STARTUPS

Think of getting a startup partner like getting a gym partner. You don't want to go? Your partner will keep you on track. Not sure how to do a particular exercise? Your partner does. You don't need a partner, but having one helps, and the statistics agree.

The key to finding a good partner is finding someone who complements your skill set. In our case, for your software company, getting someone who knows how to code is perfect: a technical cofounder. You save enormously on startup costs *and* you get all of the other benefits of having a partner.

Technical cofounders are worth their weight in gold when they're good. And they're very, very hard to get because these people get inundated a lot with offers. You know, these people can get paid $200,000 somewhere, they don't need you. And so your idea, it's crass to say it, but ideas are like assholes and everybody's got one and like you know there's even a funny blog on the internet, I don't know if it's still there, but it was a Tumblr blog called Wharton MBA Seeks Code Monkey and it was literally just a collection of Craigslist ads and stuff that were like "we have the greatest idea, it's gonna make millions of dollars and we'd love to give you 5% in exchange to build it for us" and any technical cofounder who sees that, they laugh in your face. It's like saying I have this great idea for a new building, I just need you to *build it for me. You know the idea itself is not what's important in a startup. It's always the technical deployment of it. The execution is everything. Look at Facebook. Facebook wasn't the first of its kind, not even close! It was the 7th. Friendster and Myspace and FriendFinder and all these things came before Facebook. Facebook was just better. It was smoother. It was faster. It was more controlled. It was better designed and it was better rolled out. It was MVPed and it was rolled out correctly, and that's only reason they won. It's the only reason they won. There was no other reason why they would win and I cannot even tell you how many times I've seen products that are just poorly built. And you know there's a lack of respect for technical people when it comes to non-technical people. They think their shit doesn't stink. They're so smart and they've got such great ideas and they know what they're doing and they give no respect to their technical co-founder, which is why they won't get one. If you don't get one, which more than likely you won't, because there again they're hard to find and if you find one they're gonna want to get paid. The other option is to hire and that's tough because the less you pay that's the quality of work you're gonna get. If you can afford to pay better to get more you should but even then these people are not invested deeply into the project. So sometimes it's good to find some sort of a middle ground where you pay someone to do the job and also give them a cut. And get their skin in the game, get them to care, but also don't expect people to do it for free. Even the technical co-founder is not gonna do it for free depending on how complicated it is. If it's a simple website then no big deal. But if you want some sort of app that has all the functionalities to it, it's gonna start, it's gonna get difficult.*

ILAN NASS

FOUNDER, TAKTICAL DIGITAL

Finding a Technical Co-Founder

Finding someone who wants to be your technical cofounder is not easy. The odds are stacked against you. Everyone has a software idea, but few can turn that software idea into reality. I'd wager the ratio is about 5:1.

To find this technical cofounder, you have to get out there. Leverage your existing social networks, attend events that programmers also attend, and/or make your way to the local college campus to talk with students studying computer science. Those are three ideas for you to start with. There are more. Cast a wide net to find who you are seeking. You need to! You never know who you will meet. There is no clear path to finding a technical cofounder, but if you can find one, the effort is well worth your time.

> *Go through your Rolodex. For those of you who don't know what a Rolodex is because you were born after 1990, it's like LinkedIn but on paper and only in your house. Go through your list of contacts and then reach out to people who might know people. You should know someone in your past who has built something. If your personal relationships don't work, go to meet-ups focused around the general idea and you can generally meet people. If that doesn't work, go to Angel List. But do all of these things, over and over until it works. If you take the time to do this, you will be successful.*

> **ADAM DRAPER**
> *FOUNDER, BOOST VC*

Solopreneur Checklist

You saw the statistics and you saw the benefits of having a technical cofounder. But maybe you're not so sure if you really need one, or want one. The checklist below can help you determine whether finding a technical cofounder is worth it for you and your idea in particular.

How Large is Your Idea?

If you have an idea like Uber, consider the vast number of features the app has. There are simple aspects like rating drivers and processing payments, but also complex parts like algorithms to route cars and custom GPS tracking. Even the seemingly simple aspects of Uber are expensive if you are hiring a programmer! From there, the complex features can cost an outrageous amount.

Or you can lean the other direction. In my early stages, I wanted to stay solo at all costs, so I ran with small ideas, and had to spend only a couple hundred dollars to get my MVPs made.

If you understand how much your project will cost and you have that dollar amount to invest, you can stay solo, though you may still want to find a technical cofounder. If your project is outside of your financial reach, you must find a technical cofounder, or choose a smaller idea that is within your financial reach.

Do You Have Any Experience?

Sales experience, in particular, is very important if you wish to find a technical cofounder. If you don't have any sales experience, you will have a much harder time finding a technical cofounder, because that potential partner will be far less likely to believe you can turn coding effort into money, and sales experience is quite handy if you wish to convince someone to work with you in the first place, too. Without sales experience, you may want to start as a solopreneur to get your feet wet and avoid disappointing your technical cofounder.

Do You Know Programming–at All?

With a technical cofounder, you can hand the specifics off to him and focus fully on the business part of the company. But if you are a solopreneur, you're going to want to learn the basics. I highly recommend taking at least one crash course on programming if you choose to roll solo. I know how to code, and although I do not code my own projects anymore, the knowledge is immensely helpful when dealing with my hired programmers. Without programming knowledge somewhere in you or your partner's skillset, you are in the dark.

When we fund single founders, we look for resilience and formidability. Someone that will be able to overcome both the lack of a business partner and emotional co-conspirator.

DANIEL GROSS
PARTNER, Y COMBINATOR

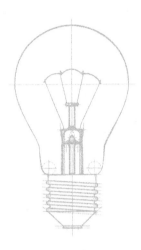

CHAPTER 5

• • • • • • • •

THE INTEGRATOR &
VISIONARY COMBINATION

A while back, one of my friends recommended *Rocket Fuel* by Gino Wickman and Mark C. Winters. This fantastic book explains the vital combination that powers many of the world's biggest and most successful companies: the visionary and the integrator. The visionary is the big-picture guy, and the integrator is the guy who makes it all work. In our software development world, the visionary is the businessman who sells the software, and the integrator is the guy who codes it.

The book struck a chord with me because when I read it, I felt like many of the pages were confirming exactly what I had already experienced myself. I tend to fail when I try to play both roles at the same time. When I program and sell, I fail, but if I just sell and leave the programming to someone else,

I succeed. I could certainly be an integrator if I had a trusty visionary at my side. But doing both just doesn't work.

To further my understanding of the topic, I emailed Mark Winters directly and explained my situation. He agreed with my assessment. You can have both programming and sales knowledge, and be either the visionary or the integrator in any project... but never both. These days, I stick to the role of Non-Technical Founder.

Apple, Microsoft, and Ford all have a visionary that we all know, but these companies also had an integrator working side-by-side with the visionary behind the scenes. You can either find a technical cofounder or hire someone to fill the role of integrator. Just don't try to do both.

Back in 2000 when I first came to Canada from Scotland, I worked at a startup where I met Rick, Justin, and Jason. The other two we met in 2004-2005 at another company we worked at called Bodog, where 5 of us worked. The others had a small agency since then. There have been lots of cross work between the six of us.

OLI GARDNER
CO-FOUNDER, UNBOUNCE

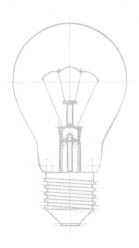

CHAPTER 6

• • • • • • • •

HIRING COSTS

You may not want to find a technical cofounder, or be able to find one even if you do. As such, you will need to hire someone to create your software for you. The next section covers all aspects of hiring a programmer, which is much easier said than done. Even if you have a technical cofounder, you should still read the following section closely, as much of the information will be of use to you when you have to work with him.

Hourly or Fixed

You can hire programmers on an hourly or fixed-price basis. Each method of hiring has its ups and downs. Neither is objectively better or worse. The ideal hiring method for you will depend on your specific circumstances.

If you can confidently describe all of the features of your idea in a 5-10 page report, along with sketches and details, then fixed-price may be your ideal method of hiring. Fixed-price tends to be more affordable because the programmer knows exactly what he is getting into. The problem is that you have never developed software before. As such, you will almost certainly leave out parts of the development process that you thought were obvious. Those parts that you thought were easy and obvious will cost extra money in the end that you have not budgeted for, which can lead to disaster.

The hourly rate is a more lenient. You describe what you need and the programmer gives you an estimate on how long everything will take. You will almost always end up paying more than the estimate, but you have far more control over the process, and you can spot potential financial setbacks before they happen, instead of paying a lump sum and getting a disastrous surprise.

I have the capability to write out complete project briefs and hire on a fixed-price basis safely, but I still choose to hire hourly. I know that hiring hourly is a gamble, as you never know how much the project will cost in the end. But I find a sense of security in paying hourly instead of a lump sum. (I'm also a lazy in a way and don't enjoy spending a week writing out such a detailed document.)

These are the major considerations you should make when deciding on hourly or fixed-price. Minor details, like worrying about hourly workers logging extra time, should not worry you at this point in the process. We aren't at the level where you should be considering those technicalities yet, though they will certainly be discussed.

It's never completely black and white. In general, the idea if you know exactly what the outcome needs to look like, if you have a spec and it's fully big and you're not really going to need to make a lot of changes then a fixed price is a good way to go. You'll get people bidding against each other and assuming that you trust the different bidders do the work, you're going to pick the one that has the right mix between cost and ability to do the work and speed at which they can deliver it. Hourly work tends to be great if you don't know exactly what you're building, which you know tends to a lot of times be the case when it's the first iteration of an app or when it's going to be an ongoing relationship. If you question about finding a technical cofounder the first person that you hire through Upwork is naturally going to be your CTO then that person is probably going to stay with you for a long time and you know you don't want to do this through a series of fixed priced contracts because you don't want to renegotiate every 3 weeks or every 3 months. You just want to say look, these are the skills I'm looking for and it's an indefinite type of contract and the number of hours per week may start pretty low and increase over time. Typically, small jobs tend to be fixed priced and big jobs tend to be hourly, so if you need a logo for your app that's probably a fixed-price job. If you need to figure out what your marketing strategy looks like or your social media strategy is or building your blog or whatever then that tends to be hourly jobs because they're ongoing and tend to be many months in a row and fairly expensive contracts. You can also go back and forth between the two. One thing that you can do is do a test project when you hire the initial 3 people for fixed price jobs that should be a few hundred bucks to find the winner and then the winner would convert from fixed price to hourly.

STEPHANE KASRIEL

CEO, UPWORK

Allow me to lead you through the real process I recently used when I hired my latest programmer. I went over to Upwork, my preferred website for hiring, and posted my ad. When the responses started flowing in, I narrowed down the applicants to those charging $10-$20 per hour. For this project, I needed only basic skills, and I knew applicants in that range could get the job done. (Expensive freelancers usually charge so much because they understand rare and in-demand programming languages and types of technology. I didn't need that for something so basic.)

Next, I checked the Upwork reviews for each freelancer in that range. I looked for bad reviews in particular. If there were any bad reviews, I did not consider the freelancer, as there were plenty of applicants with no bad reviews, and I did not see any reason to take the risk. However, I did consider applicants with no reviews, as freelancers new to any platform are often hungry for reviews, and will undercharge to secure their first clients.

Once I made a list of applicants I was interested in, I tested their command of the English language with a simple introductory interview. I asked questions like, "What similar projects have you worked on before?"

Your programmer doesn't have to speak perfect English, but it's important to reduce the language barrier. If you and your programmer understand each other, features will be built correctly the first time, which speeds up development in a significant way, and also eliminates extra hours billed when your programmer misunderstands you.

After going through the process described above, I was left with just two applicants. The first one was from Ukraine and had completed only three small projects on the platform. His bid was $12/hour. The other applicant was from Toronto like I am, just a few stops away on the subway. His bid was $15/hour. The programmer from Ukraine submitted a fairly basic application, whereas the programmer from Toronto showed a strong interest in the project and had mapped out how he wanted to do things. He even educated me on a technical aspect of the project that I was not aware of.

Still, I couldn't decide. The programmer from Toronto seemed more committed, but the programmer from Ukraine was cheaper, which can't be ignored. $12 vs. $15 can add up quickly when you start logging hours. To aid my decision, I asked for an estimate on how many hours the project would take to complete, even though I had a rough idea already, and even though I knew the estimate might not be accurate in the end.

Asking for an estimate turned out to be an excellent test of patience between the two. The programmer from Ukraine ignored my question, and instead snarkily replied if I had intentions of hiring or if I was just wasting his time, despite the fact that I had clearly hired many programmers for hundreds of hours of work already. The programmer from Toronto answered my question, and even sent me an HTML mockup of the application I was trying to build. One failed the test and one passed with flying colors. You can probably guess who did which.

I was leaning towards the programmer from Toronto, but I wanted more than a test of patience to make my decision. So I delved into the projects they had completed in a detailed way. The programmer from Ukraine had a huge number of projects completed with great reviews on each, but none of the projects were cheap ones. In fact, they were all way over my budget by a serious amount. As for the programmer from Toronto, although he had just three projects completed, each project was fairly large, and he was able to complete each one on a small budget. This behavior caught my eye, as it showed me he had worked with clients similar to myself, and he was unlikely to add in extra unworked hours when he invoiced me.

As you can probably imagine, I chose the programmer from Toronto, although I was leaning towards the programmer from Ukraine due to his cheaper fee at the start. Always do your due diligence! You can't imagine the time and money it can save you.

Though this project was hourly, I do hire on fixed-price sometimes. But, the fixed price is usually for just the core of the software, and I continue hiring the same programmer on an hourly basis to add other features after the framework is complete. This strategy allows me to be less prepared during the initial phases of the project, but still save some money on initial costs.

Prioritizing Tasks

Right now you have a big list of features you want to include in your final product, and that's great. But during your first iteration of development you will not include all of your features. You need to prioritize what you need to include at the start and what can wait until you have your first customer. Maintain your vision for the final product, but be conservative. (Make sure to include what you want to add later to your project in order to ensure the programmer you hire can handle everything. Hiring multiple programmers for one project is always more expensive and should be avoided if possible.)

Design and user interface is a big one. When people speak about MVPs they're usually talking about the number of features or what the product can do and how many options it has. That's not referencing the design or how well something is designed. If something is designed poorly it doesn't really matter what it does if no one can figure it out or becomes frustrated using it then it's on its way out the window. So having good UX and UI putting a lot of thought into the design and the polish of a product can have a big effect and that's something maybe where you wouldn't want to skimp out on. Right, whereas, you don't have to put in let's say Facebook login on the first day. You could, but that's not something that needs to happen but if people can't find the buttons or it's not intuitive or they don't know how to use it that's a much bigger problem.

ILAN NASS

FOUNDER, TAKTICAL DIGITAL

Software is a lot like a Ferrari with a Honda engine inside. The engine is very reliable, and can be manufactured quickly. But the body is what turns heads on the street. Make your engine first to get going, then add the Ferrari body once the engine is complete. This process is efficient, and an excellent business strategy.

Dealing With Programmers

Your relationship with your programmer will come down to trust. Programming ability is important, but as a Non-Technical Cofounder, you should carefully consider who you trust the most when deciding on a programmer.

There are programmers out there who will try to rip you off. Later we will discuss methods to reduce your chances of getting ripped off, but the best technique is prevention: hire a trustworthy programmer who does have a history of overcharging.

Nothing is too good to be true, especially in the world of programming. If it looks too good to be true, then it probably is. You can get a good deal, but you can't get an unbelievably good deal. Don't cut corners or you might (and almost certainly will) get burned, either by a true scammer, or someone who just delivers poor results.

The first code written for Demio was written by an outsourcing agency based in Turkey. That ended up going horribly wrong. It was a waste of 3-4 months and we ended up trashing it completely and lost about $90,000 to $100,000. That was the big wake-up call where we realized we weren't going to go with any outsourcing agency as it was too complex of a project and the technology was too complex. That's when we committed to finding *the first real team member that could come on committed for long-term. Someone that wanted to be a part of what we were building. That took us a few weeks to find that person who is still with us today.*

WYATT JOZWOWSKI

CO-FOUNDER, DEMIO

Be Highly Profitable

I like to operate under the assumption that all programmers will overcharge and go beyond my budget. This train of thought helps me prepare for the unexpected and cut out unnecessary fluff to reduce costs. Everything needs to be profitable enough where even if something goes horribly wrong in development, I still come out on top. Expect the unexpected. If everything goes off without a hitch, even better!

Hire a Proofreader

Concerned about the quality of your software, but don't have the knowledge necessary to verify anything? Hire a proofreader to run through your code line-by-line and check for any potential problems. Spending a couple hundred dollars on a qualified proofreader can help you sleep easy at night and prevent any catastrophes once your program is in the hands of your customers.

Not delivered on deadlines, lack of communication and us not being hands on enough were all signs [that this development agency was going to waste our money]. There weren't necessarily a lot of visible signs and mostly because we weren't looking for them. So if I were to redo that, even if we were to make the same mistake of hiring them, I think we could have solved it by being a lot more hands on and knowing what was going on, we would have been able to stop it earlier.

WYATT JOZWOWSKI

CO-FOUNDER, DEMIO

Your Idea Might Not Succeed

As you budget out your project, keep in mind that there is a chance that the project will not succeed and plan accordingly. Reduce costs wherever you can! You can even try to sell your MVP and earn some money from it to pay for your further feature development costs. If you do fail, don't get discouraged, because every successful entrepreneur fails a countless number of times. If you learn from your mistakes, you gain valuable knowledge, and you can apply that knowledge in the future to succeed.

Debt and Investors

I don't like debt. I don't like taking out loans and I don't like receiving outside investment. I see the long-term ramifications. If the project fails, your debt can crush you. If the project succeeds, your investors might end up snatching a massive chunk of your success away from you.

There are some projects that will require investment, and taking out a loan or finding an investor might be the only way forward. The largest "investment" I have ever received is from my friend Greg, who sent me $500 and asked only that I create the software I was considering (he was very interested in it). As such, I am biased towards not using outside capital. Still, if your project requires outside investment, I would highly recommend starting with another project that does not. Without the need for outside capital, your failures are controlled, and your successes are all yours.

People have to make these decisions on a personal level. Do I take out a loan and go into debt is one that I can't tell people to do or not do. Do I borrow money from my friends and family? Do I convince people, who know me and love me, to invest in me and if I fail can I look them in the eye? These are hard questions. These are questions that you have to ask yourself on how much you believe in your product. I personally don't. I personally will find a way. I make money at a job every day. I go to work, I make money. I could invest my own money and if I have to save up to invest I will. It's just not something I'm personally comfortable in doing. I have sought out seed investment before from professionals, professional investors, angels and such. But that's different because I can go to them with technical know-how. I can go to them with assurances with a track record. So they're more likely to invest in guys like me because I've done it before. I may partner up with a technical co-founder or an agency because a seed investor is gonna get pissed if you say that you need to raise money to go hire an agency to build this thing and the agency is gonna be the one that wins. So it's tough. And that is something that people have to make the decision on their own. More often than not though I see many founders going the friends and family route. And if you're the certain kind of person and you have a certain way of speaking and you have a good idea, your friends and family will back you, they will. They'll take a shot with you or they'll introduce you to someone who will take a shot with you. Small seed routes, if you're organized and trustworthy. I do see them more often than anything else but I don't know how comfortable I would feel personally doing it which is why I can't recommend it.

ILAN NASS

FOUNDER, TAKTICAL DIGITAL

Raising venture capital is hard. And most businesses don't raise venture investment. Unfortunately, the businesses that don't raise venture money don't get written about on TechCrunch, so a lot of founders think that startups are all about raising money. Venture money is also insanely expensive. When you do the math on venture portfolio returns (out of 10 funded startups: 7 fail quickly, 2 limp along and die slowly, and 1 exits)... so to cover the losses of the 9 out of 10 that fail, the 1 that exists needs to be at least 10x on the initial investment just to break even, at 20x you're starting to get a reasonable return for the venture partners. When you work out what it takes to return 20x over the 7 years of a typical venture fund, it's close to 80% internal rate of return. So from a startup's perspective, think about taking venture money like taking on debt that's four times more expensive than credit card debt.

PETER HUDSON

FOUNDER, SHELFIE

I'm not intrinsically against VC funding, for some startup ideas that obviously require large amounts of capital (think Uber, SpaceX), it clearly makes sense. I think many founders overly fixate on the idea of raising capital though when in fact many startups get by without just fine.

When you raise funding, you are essentially raising the bar for success. VCs are looking for a big exit so whilst a new founder might consider a few million dollars of profit each year a success, it's not enough in VC land. Your definition of success really needs to align with your investors, otherwise you should be careful about raising money. You also need to be sure there is a clear path to become a big enough company and get the exit required. For every Facebook there are many more stories of founders walking away with nothing.

JAMES BLACKWELL

CO-FOUNDER, BUZZSUMO

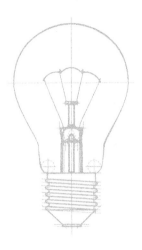

CHAPTER 7

● ● ● ● ● ● ● ●

Sources For Hiring

F inding the right programmer for your idea is essential if you wish to get your software made in an efficient manner. The following section will explain the different platforms available for you to find your programmer on, along with the ups and downs of each.

> *At the time, we weren't looking to spend a ton of money because we knew we were going to have to hire 2-3 developers, we looked on a couple freelancing sites. We found our first developer on oDesk, in addition to the second and third. Obviously those are contractors but we were lucky enough to find people that were looking for something longer term and didn't look at it like a contract project and from that point forward, we no longer looked at it like a project, but rather we are a team and we are all in this together and there really is no end. That mindset helped us find the right people.*

> **WYATT JOZWOWSKI**
>
> *CO-FOUNDER, DEMIO*

Upwork

Upwork is my #1 go-to platform for hiring and managing my programmers (and other freelancers). At its core, Upwork is a classified ad website for remote jobs. But its functionality goes far beyond an ordinary classified ad website. Everyone who applies for a job has a detailed profile with elements such as employer feedback, job success rate, and personal info (country, time zone, schooling credentials, workplace history, and more).

Upwork also handles all of the steps to hiring a freelancer within its ecosystem. The interview process is conducted through its messaging interface. Once you go through the interview process and find someone you want to hire, the project is locked in with specific project terms and conditions. From there, all hours and payment milestones are tracked, and Upwork even offers an activity tracker which takes screenshots of the freelancer's screen throughout the duration of a work session so you can ensure you are not being overbilled.

Payment processing is also handled through Upwork via an escrow system, instead of a normal third party like PayPal. This type of payment system does mean you pay some fees, but the sense of security it provides to both you and the freelancer is invaluable. Basically, by paying Upwork a small percentage of the project, you guarantee you don't get scammed outright.

Upwork is free to use (aside from the percentage-based fees), which means you are charged only when you hire someone. You can post your ad and sort through potential freelancers without paying a penny.

Overall, due to its multitude of features, Upwork has won my business, and I will be using it as an example throughout the remainder of this book.

If I were to do this again, I would go the same route of using a foreign development team and then moving domestic as the software idea validates. Just in terms of cost savings alone, it allowed a non-technical founder, myself, to be able to experiment without the heavy costs usually associated with domestic development.

JEFF MAYNARD
PRESIDENT AND CEO, BIOMETRIC SIGNATURE ID

Freelancer.com

Upwork is not the only platform of its kind—freelancer.com is another, which has similar features. In my experience, Upwork is better for hiring programmers, though I have found superior video animation designers on freelancer.com. Every platform like Upwork and freelancer.com will have its different strengths and weaknesses. If you can't find your ideal freelancer on the first platform you post your job to, try posting the same job elsewhere, and you may be surprised at the different results you get.

PeoplePerHour

PeoplePerHour takes a different approach. Freelancers are free to post "hourlies," which are pre-made offerings of services. As an example, a freelancer might offer to get your brand mentioned on Forbes for $1000. I have never hired a programmer off PeoplePerHour as the pre-made approach doesn't suit that purpose very well, but I have bought many different types of advertising from PeoplePerHour. Keep it in mind.

Fiverr

Fiverr is like PeoplePerHour, but cheaper. Fiverr started as a platform where freelancers could offer products and services for $5, hence the name. Since its inception, Fiverr has grown in a serious way, and now freelancers can offer products and services up to $1000. Personally, I have found that Fiverr has an advantage when it comes to designers. I've purchased logos for $5—$20 which would have cost $100+ (or more) on a different platform. The products and services on Fiverr are generally of a lower quality, but the prices are incredibly affordable, and that advantage keeps me coming back.

99Designs

99Designs is similar to PeoplePerHour and Fiverr, except the roles are reversed. Instead of sifting through freelancer offerings, you post your project and the freelancers come to you. You post a request for a design with a certain payout, receive dozens or hundreds of design concepts, and choose the one that you like best. For example, I posted a job for a logo with a payout of $300 and received around 300 designs from around 100 designers. Each logo was mid- to high-end (something you won't find on Fiverr). The final logo from my selected freelancer was fantastic, and my client has used it on thousands of pieces of apparel and even billboards with great success.

Forums

Sometimes, finding a programmer with specific experience relevant to your idea can be very valuable. Any programmer might be able to build a social app. But if you are building a piece of software for car dealerships, finding a programmer who has completed projects in relation to the car dealership industry can be enormously helpful. Any competent programmer can build anything if he has the proper documentation and direction, but finding someone who already knows the documentation and knows the direction he should be going in will save you a lot of headache. (Also, you might not know all the technical specifics of an industry beforehand, and a knowledgeable programmer can help you with those.)

If you search around, you can probably find a forum with the type of programmer you are looking for. As an example, if you're building a software that scans for website vulnerabilities, you might be able to find a programmer with experience in penetration testing on Hack Forums. As another, if you are creating software that helps marketers and entrepreneurs build their landing pages, maybe you find someone who already has that skill set on Warrior Forum. There are tons of forums out there, with specifics sets of people and programmers reading each one. You just have to look.

College Students

College students are hit or miss. If you can find a good college student to work for you, the benefits you receive can be enormous. But as with anything, hiring college students also comes with its drawbacks.

When I first arrived at Queen's University for my freshman year, I had some basic business knowledge, and I immediately noticed the massive source of opportunity all around me. Programmers were in abundance and no one was working on useful projects that would pay the bills. As I went along, I noticed that most first-year students didn't have the skills I needed, but second- and third-year students certainly did. These students were right in the sweet spot, where they had the programming knowledge necessary to build real software... but they had no idea how to monetize their skills. (Most students don't consider making money off their talent until they graduate and find jobs.)

Let me tell you a story of a fellow student named Otto. This kid was outstanding. He was the only one to consistently score 100% marks on the programming courses he took. He became my "unofficial intern." I would teach him concepts I had already learned myself during high school, and in return, he would work on my projects for free. At the end of our business relationship, I sent him on a round-trip vacation to Vancouver to show my appreciation, but in the meantime, I had a trustworthy and incredibly competent programmer working for me for nothing.

Finding a college student like Otto is not a walk in the park... that's why very few people consider hiring college kids. College kids are focusing on their studies and won't give you the professional hiring experience that a true freelancer would. But at the same time, college students are eager to impress, and you know they have the ability to work hard and meet deadlines, because that is exactly what schooling requires. And, since they have likely never worked for someone as a programmer, they will have far fewer expectations of you. You can make mistakes or provide incomplete information and they usually won't care, which is something to consider if you are hiring for the first time.

There is no sure fire way to find a college kid like Otto. Some corporations try to tap the potential of college students, but their approaches are broad and unfocused, which leads to poor performance and results. I have found success with taking a more personal approach. I would seek out relevant campus events and do some networking there. I would post flyers in the computer science buildings. Once I found someone who had potential, I would give him a call or meet him in person to give him a questionnaire. (I never called it an "interview." You don't want your potential programmers awkwardly showing up in suits and feeding you rehearsed answers.)

Eventually, you might be able to find someone you can work with. Unless you are a college student yourself, I would recommend seeking out third-year students in particular, as they have lots of knowledge, but they aren't in the stages where they are considering career opportunities yet.

Don't feel bad about hiring college students! Even if they work for you for free, you can provide them with references, just as I did with Otto. I let him use me as a reference, and a company he applied to work for gave me a call one day. I told them exactly what I told you in the text above, and they ended up hiring him immediately after wrapping up the phone call with me. These days, I have connections across Canada and the United States, and if I recommend someone to one of these connections, the programmer I recommend will likely get hired. Always keep in mind that college students are students, not professionals (yet).

You may come across some problems due to the fact that they are kids. One kid worked 15 hours a week on my project, but tried billing me for 30 hours, even though it was blatantly clear that he hadn't worked that much. I wasn't using Upwork, so I had to adapt to make sure I wasn't being overbilled. Still, professional freelancers will give you problems, too, and in the long run, I found that these small problems were easily offset by the cheaper (or free) work I was receiving. As long as you keep in mind that you are the only professional one in the relationship, you can make it work. Be very certain the programmer you find can complete the project in your desired time frame, then offer a lump sum that makes him want to work for you over his slightly-above-minimum-wage employer.

If you look at successful companies, there's a lot to be said about creativity but if you don't learn from all of the experience in society, that's a recipe for disaster. You somehow or another have to get experience and knowledge into your venture and recruiting a bunch of experienced managers and engineers I think is very much the important part of creating a venture.

FRANK VAN MIERLO

FOUNDER, 1366 TECHNOLOGIES

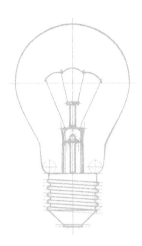

CHAPTER 8

• • • • • • • •

POSTING THE AD

9 0% of you will likely end up choosing Upwork to hire your programmer. The following section will explain how to write the ad for the job you submit. Writing a good ad is very important, as with a good one, you will receive more applicants, and each applicant will be more likely to fit the mold you need. These days, I receive heaps of applicants for every posting I make, partially because I have completed over 200 contracts on the platform, but also because my ads are written in the best way possible. Make sure to fill out your Upwork profile and verify your payment method before you start. Even without previous contracts, if you do the basics, you will get applicants with ease.

Category

Choosing your category is pretty simple. If you are building a web app, then choose web development, etc. You can browse through the development categories and pick the ones related to your project.

In general, I would strongly recommend starting with a web development, unless you specifically need the resources of a user's computer to make your software run. Web development is cross-platform and piracy protection is inherent. However, there are cases where web development is not viable, such as if you were building a piece of software to scrape emails from a list of profiles on LinkedIn. In this case, you would need lots of computational power, but more importantly, you would need more than one IP address so that LinkedIn doesn't see thousands of requests coming from your server's IP and block it. A desktop app with a feature to cycle through IPs would solve both of these problems. You also might choose desktop development if your software is complex and highly interactive (with lots of resource consumption), such as Photoshop. But in most cases, web development is superior.

Title

The title you choose will help you attract the most relevant applicants to your job, so it should be short and sweet, but completely descriptive. My most recent software project was titled, "Node.js developer for front-end and back-end development of membership website." This title showed the potential applicant that he would need to: 1) know a specific programming language, 2) design both the engine and the UI (user interface) of the website, and 3) know how membership sites functioned. This title ended up being perfect and I received dozens of qualified applicants on the first try.

Technology Stack

Note: The following text is highly opinionated! If you are a programmer, you can probably find points to argue all throughout this section, but that's the way development goes. Use my opinions as a starting point and use your own as you gain experience.

When you start, you should not restrict your programmers to certain languages or stacks of technology, because the programmer will almost always know best, though he will also be biased towards his own preferences. This bias is natural. Different programmers excel with different languages and they want to use the ones they are best with. Take the programmer's thoughts into account, but also keep in mind that you want to be able to find a similar programmer if he disappears or the project succeeds to the point where you need multiple programmers, so obscure languages and technology stacks should usually be avoided.

Programming is a fast-paced industry, so a lot of languages, even if they are popular and lots of programmers know them, could be considered non-optimal choices. Take PHP as an example. PHP is widely known and used, and it was the cornerstone of the modern web as we know it. But many other languages have surpassed PHP in functionality and usability, so even though PHP is popular, you might not want to use it.

Instead of writing an essay on the viability of an outdated language like PHP, I will give you my opinion on the technologies that will likely be popular on different platforms in the future.

Mobile is fairly simple. I recommend Objective-C and Swift for iPhone development, and Java for Android development.

When you develop for the web, you are going to need to use a stack of different languages in conjunction with each other. On the front-end, the basics are HTML and CSS, but like PHP, HTML and CSS have been updated, and HTML5 and CSS3 offer many options that the originals do not. There are also frameworks like Bootstrap, which aid in the development of websites that use HTML5 and CSS3. Finally, there are interactive languages such as JavaScript, which bases its functions off a popular library called jQuery. All of the above languages and frameworks are involved in the design (front-end) of a website, and alternatives are limited.

The back-end is different. Think of the back-end like the engine of a car, and the front-end like the exterior of a car. Most cars have similar exteriors with minor variances, but beneath the hood, everything is different. There are endless options for languages and frameworks when you develop the back-end of your website. I touched on PHP, but there are dozens, if not hundreds, of other options available.

I like freelancers who want to build in Django, which is a framework in the language of Python. Node.js has also become very popular very quickly, and Ruby on Rails has seen a similar outburst of attention and usage. You can use these recommendations as a jumping off point.

You will also need to determine how you manage your data storage, which almost all applications will need. But you should focus on your back-end development first, as data storage programming really only becomes relevant if your software takes off and has tons of data that needs to be processed. MySQL is a type of relational database and it's very popular (sort of like the PHP of data storage). MongoDB is a type of NoSQL database and also worth exploring if you reach the point where you need to focus on data storage. For now, though, you can almost always stick with the programmer's recommendation.

Lastly, we arrive at desktop development. Your main obstacle with desktop development will be the fact that Windows and Mac use different languages for their applications. Most users have Windows, but do you want to ignore Mac users completely? Maybe you start with Windows and offer Mac down the line. Regardless of platform, will users try to steal your software? Have you implemented the necessary piracy safeguards to prevent theft? You must consider all of these different questions if you choose desktop development.

Java works if you want to deploy to both Windows and Mac—its motto is "write once, run anywhere." But Java is only viable if you're not worried about piracy because other programmers can access the source code relatively easily and use your software for free. Python is the same: you can use Python on both Windows and Mac, but the source code is easy to steal. C# is a good and easy option for Windows only, and you might be able to use an option called Xamarin to automatically transform your code so it is usable on Mac, though I have no experience with Xamarin. As you can see, desktop development has many more considerations than web development does.

There is one more technology that I now require from any programmer I am considering hiring, with no exceptions. That technology is called Git. Git is a free, open-source distributed control system, which is a fancy way of saying it holds your code. Programmers upload code periodically to the repository, which can be accessed from anywhere, and you can connect the repository to your web server, where the code within can be deployed instantly. Git also assists in rolling back deployments if bugs are discovered, and there is a comment feature where programmers and savvy beta testers can tell you where problems lay.

You can certainly get software developed without using Git, but most of my own horror stories, and the horror stories I have heard from others, stem from a developer holding onto code and blackmailing the employer for access. I require Git because it removes the possibility of blackmail, which is a very real problem you may experience when you hire developers if you are not using Git or another similar type of technology.

Git is offered from many providers such as GitHub and BitBucket, and many of these providers have free options so you can take advantage of the technology without taking on additional costs as a beginner.

Description

Your description should be short. I have found that 6-10 sentences is plenty. When you write your description, you want to give out your requirements, without necessarily giving out your entire idea. Anyone can read the posting you make, and if your idea is good enough, someone might steal it.

In the first few sentences, I explain the basics I need from my programmer. For my projects, the basics usually consist of HTML5, JavaScript, PayPal IPN (instant payment notification), and web scraping. An IPN is a system used to automatically handle and process web payments, and "web scraping" is slang for data crawling/mining/etc.

I tend to not list any specifics languages as requirements, for the reasons described earlier. However, I do mention that the programmer will be required to understand and use Git. I also explain that I have a full PDF that outlines all the specifications of the project, and that they will receive this PDF if invited for an interview.

The next few sentences go over compensation. Different programmers charge different rates, so I usually don't exclude anyone based on hourly compensation alone. But, I do add a disclaimer, saying something along the lines of: "Please bid what you are worth. I don't mind paying over $18/hour, but if you request that rate, I have certain expectations for you. I expect to see productivity in every hour you log. This is a long-term project, so please treat it as such." Make sure you explain the length of your project in a realistic way. Many programmers rely on long-term projects to feed their families, so if you claim to be long-term but actually aren't, things could take a nasty turn. Honesty is key.

Lastly, I dedicate a few sentences to timeliness. Sometimes I ask programmers to tell me how long the project will take; other times I tell them how long I expect the project should take. I also include anything else related to time expectations, such as how often they should provide updates and what each update should include.

Sometimes you will find yourself hiring for positions other than programmer. For example, if you hire someone for data entry, you can easily find yourself with 100+ similar applications to a single job, regardless of size. To sort through this many applications in a time-effective manner, you need to automate some of the process. I personally create a quiz on Google Forms with about 6-8 multiple-choice questions and ask each applicant to fill out the quiz upon submitting the application. I've found that about 20% of applicants answer all questions correctly, which cuts down on time, and allows you to move forward with more confidence in the ability of each applicant who got the quiz right.

Preferred Qualifications

This section lets you specify if you have any further requirements for applicants. Your requirements will depend on your specific project. There is one universal one, though: individual or agency. Personally, I do not like hiring through an agency. You get better support through an agency (someone is always available to answer your calls or Skype messages), but I have found that agencies take forever to do the smallest tasks, and you pay more than you would if you hired an individual, too (the agency takes a cut). Individuals are cheaper because there is no middle man, and you get the opportunity to form a strong relationship with an individual, which you do not get with an agency. That being said, I know many people who prefer working with agencies, so your decision will boil down to personal preference.

You may also want to include a requirement for job success rate. Sometimes I look only at individuals with 80% or higher job success rate (100% is somewhat unrealistic). If someone completes at least 8 of 10 jobs, that applicant is almost always agreeable and understanding. You can also filter applicants by requiring at least one logged hour on the platform you are using, which may help get rid of flaky freelancers, but you also run the risk of passing over viable applicants who just joined the platform. Overall, it's really up to you. Specifying whether you want an agency or a freelancer will certainly help, but the rest is personal preference.

Be careful using any built-in qualification systems that a platform offers. For example, having a grasp on the English language is important, but the tests on any platform to certify "Good English" might be flawed. In this case, I use my own qualification system of judging the applicants based on their applications and further interview proceedings.

Screening Questions

You can save some time and headache with a few clever screening questions. You're going to receive applicants from all around the world, and because of the time zone differences, asking each interesting applicant questions might take forever. Including them on the job posting is much quicker.

One of my popular questions: "Is this the lowest price you can offer me?" This question will make applicants think twice before quoting you more than they are worth. I also ask them about when they are online (is it the same time I am?), how quickly they can begin, how long they estimate the job will take (even if I have given expectations), etc. Lastly, if my project involves an affiliate network like Clickbank or JVZoo (more on this later), I ask them if they have any experience with those platforms. Though not required, having experience is an added bonus.

Hiring on Upwork is really hard. We are fortunate enough to not have to go down that road anymore because things are doing better now. We can put out job posts on sites for people that are actually looking for careers, rather than just small projects but obviously that requires a bigger salary and more benefits that you actually have to take care of as a company. As far as finding programmers on freelancing sites, the trick is that you just have to be extremely thorough, because you can find them but it's really like finding a needle in a haystack so you just have to be really thorough and know what you're looking for, you have to be able to filter out the bad ones and you have to be willing to go through a long interview process, have tests in place that you can give them, and make sure you're hiring the right people. It's not as simple as putting up a job post, picking one of them and hoping for the best.

WYATT JOZWOWSKI

CO-FOUNDER, DEMIO

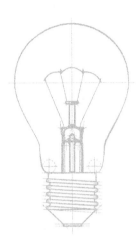

CHAPTER 9

• • • • • • • •

Picking an Applicant

Once you submit the post, you'll probably see the first applications start to flow in within the first hour. Don't get too excited and start right away, though, as you may miss the good stuff. Freelancers will be less likely to apply if they see you have already begun the interview process. I like to wait at least 12 to 24 hours before I begin.

Even if it's your first project, as long as you have followed my suggested job posting guidelines, you will have over a dozen applicants, which can be totally overwhelming. The trick to filtering out the bad ones (aside from writing a good post) is having some sort of template/filter in place to help you out.

The way it worked was Jeff Maynard and family decided that we would invest in this and so we became the investors to bankroll the company and created a couple of employees, including a CTO who was in the United States with me and Alice. What we elected to do was we selected a couple of development companies in the United States and we told them what it is we wanted and we did the same for two companies in Vietnam. After we did some research, my CTO was able to communicate effectively with them. And so we sat back and said, "okay, you guys got a couple of days each, uh give us your proposals" and the home grown guys, the development company here in the US, came back and said that can't be done and the Vietnamese, one of the groups actually showed us a demonstration of it. So in terms of the capability, we found we could do a much better job and cheaper job, in the development using outsource than we could internally.

JEFF MAYNARD

PRESIDENT AND CEO, BIOMETRIC SIGNATURE ID

Reviews and Work History

How do you predict the future? You look at the past. I usually start by archiving all of the applicants who haven't completed a task on Upwork yet. You don't have to, and you may find some motivated workers at a bargain if you don't. Upwork does provide an escrow service, so you will never get outright scammed, though the new freelancer may cut some corners if you aren't careful. That's a risk you run when you hire unvetted applicants, which is why I don't. But my work history requirements aren't too strict; one or two completed jobs with perfect reviews on each is usually enough for the applicant to make it to the next round.

Job Success Rate

Half-finished projects are a pet peeve of mine. Upwork recently started displaying a metric that tells you how many jobs the applicant has taken on vs. how many were actually completed. If the project success rate is below 80%, I almost always cross that applicant off the list. If I have many applicants, sometimes I look at only 90% and above. The project success rate will heavily influence the success rate on your project, but be sure to watch out for freelancers who are more pushy to mark a contract as completed to boost this metric on their profiles.

Skills

The more skills an applicant has, the better. Back in high school I didn't understand this fact completely. I hired a PHP developer. As it turned out, he knew only PHP and nothing else. He was unable to deploy the code to my server... he said he needed a drag-and-drop interface!

You'll want to look for full-stack developers, or as close to them as you can get. These days, colleges and universities are churning out almost exclusively full-stack developers, so they are much easier to find than before. A full-stack developer understands the front-end, the back-end, databases, servers, and more. The acronym LAMP (Linux, apache, MySQL and PHP, Python, or Perl) describes it perfectly. (Apache is an open-source HTTP server that allows web browsers to connect to your server. Developers who can configure some sort of HTTP server, whether that is Apache or Nginx, are very handy.)

Communication

Now you are going to start messaging the applicants you haven't crossed off the list. Most won't respond. If they don't respond, cross them off the list, too, especially if you message them during your work day. Communication is key. Your ideal programmer expresses interest, makes himself available, and is eager to begin.

For everyone who does respond, make sure they have a decent grasp of the English language. Keep in mind that you will likely be dealing with programmers who do not have English as their first language, so it might not be perfect, but you need to ensure that they can understand you when you express what you need. Once you get a couple messages back from the applicant, you should be able to judge his communication ability pretty well. Once you get rid of the applicants who don't have good English, you should have around three to six shortlisted applicants that you can focus on.

When hiring, there's a lot of people that we've come into contact with that everybody says they can do it, whatever task it is. But you have to lay out certain very big specifics when you're in the development phase. You can't

just assume there's any gray area because that gray area will be where they interpret something and you'll find that your project will get off track.
JEFF MAYNARD
PRESIDENT AND CEO, BIOMETRIC SIGNATURE ID

The Phone Call

When I'm hiring for a long-term position, one of the first things I do is give each potential applicant a call. I'm also a big believer in weekly phone calls to recap progress that has been made, and there's no better way to do that than to start with an initial phone call. I didn't use the phone in the past, but now I do, and I have had increased success when hiring because of it.

You could say that the telephone is what separates the men from the boys, figuratively speaking. People hate talking on the phone if they are going to rip you off or waste your time. Just the idea of a phone call can be enough to weed out the bad apples.

A lot of your applicants won't be able to take your phone call because they do not have a good enough grasp on the English language. If that's the case, do you cross them off the list, or be understanding as to their situation? Personally, I cross them off the list, because although they may be excellent people with fantastic programming ability, communication is essential to the continued success of my ventures.

Phone calls also help you establish a connection (or lack of a connection) that you can't do through text, which can also assist in your "gut feeling," explained a bit further below.

Price

If you post a project without specifying an hourly rate, you'll likely have bids between $12 to $50 per hour. That situation is completely normal. I tend to hire in between the $12 to $20 per hour range, as I have found that range provides the best value (the programming I need without the exorbitant price tag). But, if this is your first time hiring a programmer, you will probably want to lean a bit higher than that, because with higher price points, you get more savvy programmers, who cannot just write your code but guide you towards doing things in the correct and most efficient way as well. If you get to the point where you need a second developer for the same project, you can lean back towards the cheaper rates, because you already have the guidance you need from your first, more-expensive programmer.

Project PDF

At this step in the process I normally have two to four applicants remaining. One might stop responding in a timely manner or lose interest, so you can cross him off the list. Send the PDF to anyone who you deem acceptable and who has kept up with your standards of communication.

Once you send it, you want to see who takes the time to actually read it. If an applicant says "ok, when can we start?" that's a bad sign. You want someone who takes the time to read your PDF and ask questions about it. Though it may seem counterintuitive, you want to pick the freelancer who says that your project is difficult, not the one who says it is easy. If a programmer says it's easy, he probably hasn't read the PDF carefully. Few programming projects are truly "easy."

Gut Feeling

At this point you have one or a few applicants who all fit your criteria and you just can't decide. My method to get over this indecisiveness is to sit on the project for a full day. If anyone flakes on you during that time, cross him off the list. But chances are that no one will flake, seeing as they have all kept up to your communication standards during this entire process. You're going to have to rely on your gut feeling. Who do you feel you have the best connection with?

Think with the intention of forever. According to Warren Buffet, choosing who you plan to marry is the "single most important decision" you will ever make. Spending a long time with the wrong person can be very, very bad. Think of your applicant in the same way as you would a potential partner for marriage. You want to pick someone who you will feel comfortable with for a long time. Trust your gut to make the final decision for you, if you have to.

Starting the Contract

Finally, you're all set! Now is when you should set up your Git repository and send over the login details. Always make sure you own the Git repository yourself. Just add the programmer to the repo and grant him read and write access rights. You'll likely have to buy a server before you can start with Git.

At this point, you should also discuss progress updates (before the work begins). For most of my staff, I simply ask them to keep me updated on progress, but some of you may prefer updates on a regular basis. The good news is that Upwork provides tracking, comments, and screenshots for all hours worked, so you can double-check that these updates are in fact truthful.

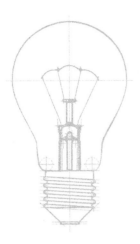

CHAPTER 10

• • • • • • • •

SWITCHING TO HOURLY

f you are using a fixed-price contract, once the programmer has successfully implemented everything agreed upon in the PDF you sent over, you want to thoroughly test the features before marking the contract as complete. You want to make sure you received what you paid for. If bugs exist, the programmer will fix them, but if you mark it as complete and bring up bugs after the fact, you are being unreasonable by asking him to work for free.

If your fixed-price contract goes off without a hitch, switch your contract to hourly, because you will very likely have further work that needs to be done on the project, and you are always better off sticking with one programmer whenever possible.

Communicating

Especially with an hourly contract, you are going to want to be in regular communication with your programmer to ensure everything is on track, and if you followed my guidelines for posting your job, you should have already outlined these expectations clearly.

Calls are, in my opinion, the single best way to communicate, which is why I recommended ensuring that you can communicate with your programmer over the phone. I also use Skype and Facebook Messenger in some cases, because phone calls have the potential to eat up a lot of time. Aside from the actual communication, you will need to stay organized. I use Trello to keep my sanity. I create a single board and invite my programmers to participate. The board consists of five columns, each with cards which represent a bug, feature, or idea. The columns I create are as follows:

On hold. This column contains new ideas that I haven't budgeted for yet. In general, this column exists only before you get your first customer. After your first customer, everything from this column is shifted to the next.

Unassigned. This column contains features, bug fixes, and ideas that are waiting for implementation. When a programmer is ready for a new task, he can claim it by moving a card from this column to the next.

In-progress. When a programmer has claimed a task, the card appears here. This column gives me a good overview of what is being worked on.

Pending approval. Once a programmer completes the task he has claimed, he moves the card to this column and I verify that it works properly and as expected. About 50% of the time, the task is only partially complete, so I add a comment to the card and move it to the previous column. The programmer gets a notification that the card has not been approved and works on fixing it.

Complete. If a card is completed and verified, it is then shifted to this column. Trello keeps tabs on who has interacted with a specific card, along with any notes on the card, so if anything goes wrong in the future, I know who is responsible.

Trello is unbelievably useful to me. I can manage my entire team at a glance, and everyone gets notifications when anything happens so there are minimal delays in development.

My partner David is more organized with this stuff and he focuses more on systems. Everybody is in Slack as far as communication. We use Trello for project management and we have different boards for development, bugs, and features as we try to separate all that stuff. We do daily sprints and we have team members report what they want to get done for the day and at the end of the day, what they got done. Then we do weekly meetings, via Demio, to start the week and what our goals are as a team and give updates on what's going on in the company. For the most part, we don't try to micromanage as everybody has their own space they specialize in but just make sure everyone is up to date. We all follow the same processes. We start to get a lot of users since each customer has perhaps 1000 attendees so it's our job to not overwhelm the team when bugs come up. What really matters to a lot of us is prioritization and strategizing how we are going to attack new features and bugs.

WYATT JOZWOWSKI
CO-FOUNDER, DEMIO

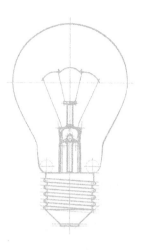

CHAPTER 11

• • • • • • • •

BETA TESTING

n the software world, stages of development are explained by the Greek alphabet. When a project is first completed by a programmer and you start going through it, you are in the alpha build. There are probably a ton of bugs to the point where the software is unusable. Once you figure out the kinks as best as you can, you enter the beta phase, and start finding people to test your software.

Your beta testers can come from all over. I usually crowdsource finding beta testers by letting a few people from forums use it for free. In other cases, I have called on friends in the industry (or even just friends from school) to test it out. People are usually happy to help!

The entire user process must be tested. So if your software is for sale, you need to have your beta testers actually buy it. Usually, I send each beta tester the cost of the software on PayPal, then the beta tester refunds it after the purchase is complete so no money is lost in PayPal fees.

Beta testers have the ability to create bug reports in the Git repository, which my programmer can then respond to and fix. This process makes the entire beta testing process virtually hands-off for me. I just view the logs to see what is happening at my leisure.

Nielsen's 10 Usability Heuristics for User Interface Design

You're going to have to test quite a lot during the beta phase of your software. One of the most important parts is the UI (user interface). Believe it or not, some of the most widely-used software is coded terribly, but because the UI is so fantastic, the bugs are hidden from the user's view when they do occur.

I learned about Jakob Nielsen's 10 Usability Heuristics during my time spent studying at the University of Toronto. I strongly urge you to familiarize yourself with these concepts and mark this page for later use. You can also look up the full original article by Jakob Nielson on the Nielsen Normal Group website, which has explanatory information to accompany each heuristic.

- Visibility of system status.
- Match between system and the real world.
- User control and freedom.
- Consistency and standards.
- Error prevention.
- Recognition rather than recall.
- Flexibility and efficiency of use.
- Aesthetic and minimalist design.
- Help users recognize, diagnose, and recover from errors.
- Help and documentation.

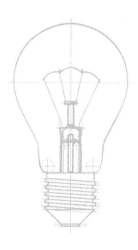

CHAPTER 12

• • • • • • • •

BE SAFE, PROTECT YOURSELF

Building trust with someone, who you have never met, is difficult. Give your programmers as much leeway as you would a random person on the street. If something smells fishy, hold your ground. I have been scammed many times by many different people. So has virtually every other entrepreneur in the world. (I don't get scammed very much anymore, as I can smell them from a mile away these days, but at the start, you will not have this 6th sense.)

Upwork provides Escrow milestones for you to use. USE THEM! Break your project into chunks of 20%. Be fair when releasing milestones, but also make sure your programmer is being fair in return. For the first couple milestones, you may have a hard time grasping how much work has or has not been done, but by the halfway mark, you should be able to realistically see if your project is on track to be completed successfully.

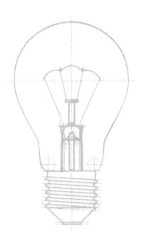

CHAPTER 13

• • • • • • • •

MAINTAINING GOOD RELATIONSHIPS

D on't let your emotions get in the way of business. I cannot stress this enough! Emotions are usually amplified over text because the receiver of the text has no context or tone to read. I've worked with some fairly manipulative programmers, but because I separated emotion from business, I always ended things in a civil and peaceful manner, even if I did not believe they deserved such a courtesy. Nothing good can come of letting your emotions run wild.

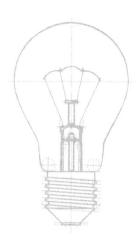

CHAPTER 14

• • • • • • • •

DEVELOPING THE MISCELLANEOUS

Your software business consists of more than just software. You need a few other things to tie everything together.

You will need a logo. You can start with a cheap logo from Fiverr. I pay $5 or $10 for my starting logos. If the project is successful, I head over to 99Designs and pay around $300 for a better logo. Don't worry about starting with a cheap logo. If you hunt around Fiverr, you'll be surprised at the quality you can get for just a couple bucks. (Nike paid $35 for its logo.)

In most cases, you will also need a website aside from your landing page(s). If you are developing a mobile app, you can get by with a simple website with a single page. All you really need to put on that page is a link to the app and a contact form. If you are developing anything other than a mobile app, you will need a full website with multiple pages. For full websites, WordPress is your best friend. As we touched on earlier, WordPress is a content management system that is easy to pick up, even if you have zero technical or design experience. Get your domain name, install WordPress, and get cracking. I have a free six-part video course available on YouTube that can help you understand WordPress, and there are many other resources out there as well. (WordPress is the most popular content management system, so whenever you need help, you will be able to find it.)

Once your logo is designed and your website is up and running, a smart next step is getting your website to the top of Google for your brand name and other relevant keywords. You can buy SEO (search engine optimization) "services" from SEO forums to help with this step. I try to maintain an updated list of good SEO services on my blog (joshmacdonald.net). Aside from using my recommendations, you can help yourself pick good services by looking at real reviews that customers have provided.

Those are the basics. You may want to get other business assets like business cards. For business cards, use Fiverr for the design, and get them printed via VistaPrint. This approach lets you equip yourself with what you need without spending a fortune. Use the same strategy for other business assets you think you want or need. Save money whenever possible, because you are just starting. (We will cover more complicated marketing strategies like pay-per-click advertising in later chapters.)

You should also put together text and/or video guides to help your customers get started using your software. You know your software in and out, but your customers do not, and you would be surprised how many people will struggle with the seemingly basic aspects of it. With helpful initial guidance and a detailed FAQ page (many of your customer questions will be the exact same), you can save yourself a ton of time on customer support. A good rule of thumb is to treat every customer like an 8-year-old. Extra documentation never hurts.

PART 3

• • • • • • • •

The Marketing Stage

A t this point you have hit the ground running with development. Development can take forever, so your best bet is moving forward while your programmer works on the product. In the early stages of development, you need to commit just an hour or so every day to answer questions and review progress updates.

I have worked in business-to-business and my whole life has been business-to-business and so you find customers by talking to people. You just go visit people. It's just classic, old-fashioned sales. As a friend of mine says, "most problems can get solved in 50 phone calls or less." Most of all there's a willingness to climb on a plane and go visit people. Sales is a continuum and on one end you're selling Boeing aircrafts and if you're selling Boeing aircrafts then the president of the United States is going to help you close those sales because if you sell 20 Boeing aircrafts then it's a huge amount of jobs for the country and it's very important. The guy who ultimately closes the sale is the president of Boeing. You tend to sell to heads of state. That's one extreme. The other extreme you're selling toothpaste and you can't do any customer contact because it's like $3 for a tube of toothpaste or whatever it is. Then it's all about marketing and it's a completely different scenario, and so my business has always been a number of very large contracts. If you supplier with silicon wafers then they will sign a $700 million contract and for those things you fly to Germany and you go and meet those guys. Then they have a colleague elsewhere and you fly there and meet them and that's how you do it.

FRANK VAN MIERLO

FOUNDER, 1366 TECHNOLOGIES

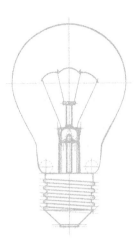

CHAPTER 15

· · · · · · · ·

WEBSITE

We have covered the basic steps to building a website. Don't wait. Start building your website now. I gave you instructions on creating the website in earlier chapters (domain, hosting, WordPress). Go back and follow those instructions. Once you have your website set up, you may want to consider purchasing a paid WordPress theme for your website. A paid WordPress theme makes your company look professional instead of amateur. ThemeForest and TemplateMonster are good resources to find paid themes (each one costs between $20 to $60, not nearly as much as hiring a designer costs). As for what to put on your website, just look at your competitors. You don't have to reinvent the wheel. See which pages they have, copy them, and your website is complete.

Sales Copy

Now you need to start putting stuff on your website. The main focus of any business website is the sales copy. You want to write sales copy that prompts visitors to take your desired action (buy or download your software). This type of persuasion is called copywriting, and it is an artform. You can read books to improve your copywriting ability. We will cover the basics below.

Understanding Your Audience

Your selling points should revolve around what your buyer wants and is looking for. Imagine you are trying to sell the latest cell phone. Your sales copy will not be the same for everyone. You will want to include different selling points if you are selling to a middle-aged businessman vs. a freshman-year college student. What convinces businessmen to buy will not convince college students, and vice-versa. Understanding who is reading your sales copy is the first step to good copywriting.

Clear Explanations

Realize that your visitors are impatient. You need to convey a lot of information very quickly in an easy-to-understand way. Even if you have the best software, if you can't explain why it is the best, no one will care. They will just close the page and move on with their lives. With clear and concise salesmanship, even if the visitor does not buy right then and there, he will know what your product is about and why it is the best, and he may decide to return to your website and make a purchase later on.

Videos

A video makes it easy for you to convey a lot of information to the visitor quickly. However, explanatory videos are expensive, and not needed unless you have an exceptionally complex product and/or you are getting a lot of traffic and want to improve your conversion rates. If your software can be explained with text and images easily enough, choose that route for now, and consider making an explanatory video down the line.

Value Proposition

Newbies often believe they need to show a creative slogan or a list of statistics at the top of their website. Wrong, wrong, wrong! Unless you are a Fortune 500 company that is recognized globally, you must begin with a value proposition. A value proposition quickly and effectively explains what your product is and how it can help.

Ensure you put your value proposition above the fold. On a website, anything above the fold is what the visitor can see without needing to scroll down. A visitor won't scroll down unless you capture his attention, which you can do with a value proposition. Once the visitor understands the value he can receive from your software, he may continue scrolling, and you can add things like statistics further down.

Thinking of your value proposition can be tough. Look at big companies if you are having difficulty. Companies like Apple and Stripe have value propositions mastered, as they employ the best and brightest copywriters around. You can also look at my amazing guest contributors like Unbounce, Hotjar, and Demio. Their value propositions are equally fantastic, and probably closer to the value proposition you will be offering for your software.

Reviews, Testimonials, And Quotes

Humans are social creatures. As such, social proof is one of the easiest ways to convince your visitors to take an action. Ask your beta testers or early buyers for a few sentences of feedback in exchange for a discount or other perk. Proudly display these testimonials on your website.

As a music publisher, our "clients" are artists and writers. As in any company/ client relationship, it is all about trust. How do you develop that trust? Well, as you say, you have to start with a first. So that means you have to have enough knowledge and charisma to have someone "take a chance" on you to start. Once you do that and assuming you do a great job for the first client, in my business anyway, additional clients tend to come from word of mouth and the clients you target on your own often have links to you original few clients, so they then provide good references. Have a look at our testimonials page. That is a CRITICAL tool for us as a newer brand.

I find so many people have so little time that a good word from a trusted source goes much further than cold calls or blind meetings. An example for me is that we'd have never been able to sign John Legend if will.i.am from the Black Eyed Peas didn't endorse us. EVERYONE was hunting John, and Will just said, "These guys are great. You should go there. I trust them."

RICHARD STUMPF
FOUNDER, ATLAS MUSIC GROUP

Consider the Length

A big copywriting mistake is writing too much text. I find myself making this mistake all of the time. Giving your visitor lots of information is good, but you have to do it in a creative way. For longer sections, give the visitor the option to show/hide chunks of text, and always be looking to say more with less.

Concentrate Above the Fold

Above the fold is the most important part of your website and can make or break the sales effectiveness of it. Concentrate on everything above the fold first and foremost, as most of the decisions a visitor makes will be based upon what he sees first. The last thing you want to do is greet your visitor with a wall of text or random image.

Create a Clear Call-to-Action

Your CTA (call-to-action) is arguably the most important element on your entire website. You must make it clear what action the visitor can take to continue down his path after he has finished going through your website. For example, your CTA can be an invitation to make a purchase, start a free trial, or download something.

Since your CTA is so important, you want it to stand out. The eyes of your visitors should flick to your CTA right away. I use a simple method to determine if my CTA is noticeable enough. I hold my pointer finger a few inches away from my eyes and focus on it so the website becomes blurry but I can still see the overall shape and flow of the elements. If I can clearly tell where the CTA is, then I know it's good. If I can't, I adjust the design elements of the CTA, such as color, size, and spacing in relation to other design elements on the page. The design of the CTA is just as important as the text on the CTA.

Do not rush your CTA. CTAs are so powerful that many ad networks will not allow you to advertise with images that contain CTAs. Be sure to leverage the power they hold to your advantage.

Track Everything

You never know how your website is performing unless you look at visitor activity. You can use a service like hotjar.com (free) to create a heat map of visitor activity, which shows you where visitors are scrolling to, what they are focusing on, and what they are clicking on. Use your heatmaps to improve your website's performance.

A/B Testing

You determine how well your adjustments are working with a process called split testing (also known as A/B testing). You start with your original website. Then you make a change, and send visitors to each page equally, and see which version performs better. With split testing, you know for certain if any adjustments you made are beneficial to you or not. You can use a service like Optimizely to simplify your split testing process, though Optimizely is somewhat expensive, so you may want to shop around.

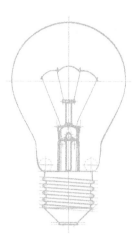

CHAPTER 16

• • • • • • • •

PRICING

There are a number of important decisions you have to make in regards to your software before you can begin calling it a product. One of these decisions is how much you charge. You will want to price your product based on your standing in the market. Personally, if I am well-known in the market, I will charge much more than my competitors. But if I'm not, and especially if my product does not contain all of the features of similar existing products, I will charge less than my competitors so that I can get noticed.

I've seen startups start their pricing too low, have to raise it and then piss off existing customers in the process. When people buy in to what you are doing early, they want to be rewarded. So, it's better to start with a high price and give a discount to early customers to establish the value, and then maybe have the discount expire after a certain time or grandfather in early customers to give you more flexibility. Start higher and move lower if needed, not the other way around.

CAROL ROTH

TV CONTRIBUTOR AND BEST-SELLING AUTHOR

If you are new to a market, consider offering a free trial option if it is a good fit for your software. Microsoft Office offers a 30-day free trial option. If the user likes the software, he will likely want to continue using it, and make the purchase. In this case, free trials work great. However, if your software is more of a one-time-use product, such as a file conversion software, then free trials might not work as well, because the user will just download the free trial, use the software, have no further need for it, and never make the purchase.

Free trials are particularly effective because you will usually have customers who are interested in your product, but not interested enough to reach out to support and ask pre-purchase questions. Live chat can help with potential customers like these ones, but free trials are a hands-off way to get them under your wing. Free trials also lower your refund rate because customers know exactly what they are getting when they make the full purchase. There are a lot of good reasons to offer a free trial if you can, and I highly recommend doing so.

When you start off, you're afraid no one is going to pay for it, always, so a lot of people price low. On the low end, we'd get people who just wanted to put up a webpage. We would get 80-year-old retirees who just wanted to get on the internet. There was this old guy Lamar, who would call every day, I think he was lonely, and it just kills your support. Support spends so much time explaining just what marketing is. It was terrible. It sucks up your time. They then leave so your metrics are bad and your support cost is high. So what we ended up doing then is looking at analytics and chopped off our lowest price point which were the $10 and $25 plans. The revenue went up and a lot of the people who aren't your target market drop off. Support wasn't as busy and they could focus on our real customers. Then overtime, that keeps happening. So we just did that again, we knock off our bottom tier and switched by default to annual billing, so our cash has gone up *massively because a lot of people are choosing annual billing, which is great for a startup because having a lot of cash in the bank can be really valuable and it has been a dramatic effect for us.*

I was at MarketingProfs' B2B Marketing Forum which is a conference and I was at one of the booths and people would come by and people would say, "Ya ya ya, we know that product, but they're too cheap so we can't use it." Some bigger companies have staff that can't justify to their boss when something is too cheap. They're paying $12,000 per month for this or $5,000 per year for that and they see $99 per month and think, "well $99 per month, that can't be good or that can't be secure." Pricing is really interesting when you decide who you're selling to.

We always offered annual pricing manually, but since we switched it on automatically, it has had a dramatic effect.

OLI GARDNER
CO-FOUNDER, UNBOUNCE

———————

Our pricing model is quite simple. It's based basically on our costs, which some people might say is not the cleverest thing to do but we believe in building awesome technology and putting it into the hands of everyone. So, the more traffic you have, the more data you want to collect, the more expensive it becomes. If it's more expensive for us then we charge you more. On our pricing page you can see it starts 89 Euros or 89 dollars and it scales all the way up to over 1000 per month and then there's scale up recordings. You can have always-on recordings but that's not yet available, it's still on kind of internal beta. So yeah, some of our customers do pay much larger amounts but the higher data collection rate is a relatively new thing, we're in the initial phase of that.

DR. DAVID DARMANIN
CO-FOUNDER, HOTJAR

———————

Taktical Digital has gone through a number of iterations with pricing just because it's kind of hard to price out marketing. Sometimes you want to charge a percentage of spent on the ad budget, sometimes you want to charge a flat monthly, sometimes you want to charge hourly. Different clients have different preferences, and different services have different needs. So as an agency it's really hard to price, and I've struggled with that a lot over the years. I've changed my pricing from high to low to high to low multiple times. But one example of a company that screwed up their pricing big time was a client/company that we're dealing with the failure of, right now. We did $1.3 million in sales for this company and they're going under. And they're going under because they charge $60 a month for their product when everyone else in their space is charging $88 per month. This was a supplement company. First of all, it was insane to me that these people didn't check. That no one even knew what the standard pricing in the industry was. They ran sales for a long time and then only found out later that the subscription was undervalued and now they don't have enough money to cover their costs. They're in debt a couple hundred grand and they can't get out of it. So my advice is always start your pricing low. You can always raise your prices. Always. But if you lower your prices, you're gonna make some of your customers angry. If someone sees they paid more and the price went down, they're gonna come back and demand refunds. Whereas starting your price off low you can get some customers in the door. But very quickly start experimenting with raising that price. Do not allow 6, 8, 10 months and $1 million in sales to go by before you realize, holy crap, I'm not making a profit here. Do your research, especially in subscription companies because that's the hardest one. Subscription models are very hard to price because it's not just about getting someone in the door the first time, it's about keeping them long-term. So you do have to experiment. And that's what betas are for, that's what soft launches are for. It's about gauging the market. Start your prices off low, get some customers in the door and then start tweaking it *up slowly, slowly, slowly. And eventually you will find the pricing that is the best, the optimal pricing.*

ILAN NASS

FOUNDER, TAKTICAL DIGITAL

Recurring VS. One-Time

When you sell a product, you have two overarching choices when it comes to charging your customers money. You can charge a fixed price for lifetime access to the product, or you can charge a monthly fee for continued access to the product. All products in the world fall into these two categories. When you buy a boat, you probably pay a lump sum to own your boat forever, but if you need to buy a space on a dock for your boat, you probably pay a monthly or yearly fee for continued access to that space.

In 2017, we live in a subscription economy. Take Netflix as an example. Netflix changed an entire industry by recognizing that people preferred to pay a monthly fee to access movies and TV shows rather than a fixed-price fee to rent or own movies and TV shows.

The recurring model has a whole lot of benefits. People pay whether they use the product or not. Many people don't take the time to cancel their memberships. The monthly fees from both active and inactive customers help you maintain the software and keep your cash flow steady. And increasing your number of monthly subscribers helps your eventual valuation, which we will cover later on. (For now, all you need to know is that internet businesses are usually valued on a multiple of their monthly net profits.)

But the fixed-price model does have its benefits as well. You can quickly make more because your fixed price is the equivalent of many months of recurring fees. Hypothetically, you can sell a piece of software, make a bunch of money, and forget about it. But things are rarely so simple. What you need to keep in mind if you charge a fixed price is that unless you specify a limit on the support you will provide, customers will expect the software to work forever, which puts you in a tricky situation. If you keep updating the software without a steady influx of new customers, you might bankrupt your business. On the other hand, if you don't update your software, you will have broken your promise to your customers, and just a few angry customers can have a significant effect on your reputation.

I learned this lesson the hard way. I saw the opportunity to make short-term money and I sold lifetime licenses of Keyword Scout without considering the long-term ramifications. Learn from my mistakes! If you do decide to go the fixed-price route, make sure you specify how long you will support the product for. Or, charge monthly and provide a discounted option for yearly licenses so you can't shoot yourself in the foot.

Payment Processors

Payment processors are like any other technology—they come and go. We'll cover a few of the most popular options right now, but you should do your due diligence to make sure these options are still the best whenever you are reading this book.

PayPal

PayPal had an atrocious reputation up until about 2012, but since then, the company has cleaned up its act in a big way (at least in my experience). The support division seems to be improving steadily. More importantly, buyers trust PayPal, and trust is very important whenever a customer is thinking about entering his credit card info to make a purchase. PayPal has very reasonable processing fees, but very unreasonable currency conversion fees. If you live in Canada and want to use PayPal, try to register a bank account with US currency to withdraw your money into, then use the bank to convert your currency, not PayPal.

There are two primary disadvantages with PayPal that you should be aware of. The first disadvantage is that certain countries cannot make payments through PayPal, which isn't a problem if you are selling to people only in the US. But if you are selling globally, you will lose some customers if PayPal is your only payment option. The second disadvantage is PayPal's dispute system, which heavily favors the buyer. As the seller, you will likely lose your disputes through PayPal, even if you are in the right. (Some buyers are aware of this favoritism and will abuse the dispute system in an attempt to get your software for free.)

I use PayPal at the time of writing this book, but I'm not dedicated to the company. As soon as I have a solid track record with another option, I will strongly consider not using PayPal.

2Checkout

I have had nothing but bad experiences with 2Checkout. That being said, I know people who swear by 2Checkout, so they are on the list. 2Checkout allows you to accept PayPal payments without having a PayPal account of your own. And, they have the option to receive payment to a prepaid credit hard, which was very helpful to me in my younger years before I had a real credit card.

Clickbank

Clickbank tends to process payments for high-risk products. As such, they have high fees. But you can accept payments for almost anything with Clickbank when other companies might turn you down. Clickbank has a huge marketplace of products and an internal affiliate system. You can set a percentage to pay out to affiliates when they make sales, and if your landing page is any good, affiliates might start promoting your product for you.

JvZoo

JvZoo is similar to Clickbank in that they have a large network of affiliates that might promote your product. However, unlike Clickbank, you must have a PayPal account to use JvZoo. Payments are made directly to your PayPal account. Fees for JvZoo are lower than Clickbank, but higher than PayPal, because the ecosystem is built on top of PayPal and its fees.

Bitcoin

Bitcoin has some advantages but a few very annoying disadvantages. One major advantage is that transactions are not reversible no matter what, so a scammer can't dispute the payment or chargeback the payment on his credit card. But, there is no way to reliably accept recurring payments, because even if you use a processor like CoinBase to automatically try to receive them, that strategy relies on the customer having enough bitcoin in his CoinBase wallet (if the wallet is empty, you can't get paid).

Stripe, Payza, Skrill, PerfectMoney

There are many other payment processors out there. Stripe has excellent reviews, but I have just started to test it out, so I can't speak to its quality. Skrill and PerfectMoney are other interesting options, as they both work in a higher number of countries than PayPal does, and they do not favor the buyer so heavily in disputes like PayPal does. One or more of these options may be a perfect fit for your business; explore them yourself in order to make your decision.

I've heard some horror stories with PayPal. PayPal has held back thousands of dollars of my money in the past. Fraud is rampant among payment processors and they're always looking out for it. There's really no very good solution. Payment processing is tough. I like Stripe right now, I'm a fan. But if something goes wrong in your billing, if a hacker steals credit cards and buys up product or something along those lines and you get 500 chargebacks on your credit card statements and they shut you down or they withhold your cash, you're at their mercy. So payment processing is a real problem, that's why bitcoin and blockchain is such a big deal right now. Banks can crush you and PayPal is a bank and if they wanna crush you for whatever reason, they don't like the way you do business or something they can crush you and destroy your business. So being careful is important but I don't know if one payment processor is going to be able to save that from happening.

ILAN NASS

FOUNDER, TAKTICAL DIGITAL

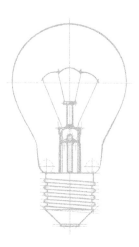

CHAPTER 17

• • • • • • • •

UPSELLS

An upsell is a product that you attempt to sell to buyers who have already purchased your main product. Downsell is another term, which means the same thing as upsell, except an upsell is more expensive than your main product, and a downsell is less expensive.

Upsells can be extremely profitable if the upsell is a good fit as a follow-up to your main product. In fact, some businesses rely heavily on upsells in order to be profitable. Various software companies sell cheap software around $10 and bank on a small percentage of users purchasing the upsell, which may cost hundreds of dollars.

The only limit to your upsells and downsells is your imagination. If your software requires self-education to use, you could attempt to push an upsell that offers one-on-one coaching on how to use the product to its fullest potential. Or, you could turn that upsell into a downsell, and offer an advanced manual with the same information you would explain in a one-on-one session for a cheaper price. The sky's the limit.

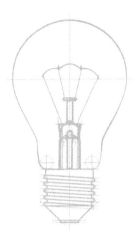

CHAPTER 18

• • • • • • • •

DIFFERENT VERSIONS & PLANS

Software products have many opportunities to maximize revenue. You could offer different versions of the software to different types of customers. For example, you could offer a limited, affordable solution for mom-and-pop shops, and a robust, expensive solution for large corporations. Both of these customers have different needs and budgets, so you would be wise to cater to their needs and try to expand your customer base. Once you identify your market, you can think of different versions of your product that you might try offering.

CHAPTER 19

• • • • • • • •

THE FASTEST WAYS TO GROW

Now that you have made the bulk of the businesses decisions, you have arrived at the part where you start thinking about getting your first customers. (You may decide to revisit the decisions you have made after you talk with your first few customers.)

There are countless ways to get your first customers, but let's talk about the best ways first. In my opinion, the single best way to get your first customers is by working with someone who has existing relationships with potential customers. There are two types of people that fit this definition. You can form a partnership and make sales through cross-promotion and integration, or, you can get affiliates to promote your product for you, and give the affiliate a cut of each sale that he makes.

I was struggling to get any job interviews, as I had mentioned and my job skills in Hollywood did not translate to the entertainment industry in New York. I was just trying to find a job when a friend, who was producing a

Broadway show, called me and said they were looking to make a switch from their digital agency and asked if I was interested in coming in to talk about it. I said sure. The friend was producing a show on Broadway and it wasn't selling tickets, which is kind of important with a Broadway show and long story short, they needed to bring in some new blood and new ideas and that's how it came about.

ADAM CUNNINGHAM
FOUNDER, 87AM

Mutualism

Crocodiles often get meat stuck in between their teeth, which causes them pain. So, plover birds sit inside the mouths of crocodiles and pick the meat from their teeth. The plover bird gets a free meal and the crocodile gets his teeth cleaned. The two animals have created a mutually beneficial relationship. Everyone wins.

Here's another example, this time, with humans. My friend Brad owns a company called NeverBounce. His software cleans large email lists for large corporations. Imagine a cashier offers you a 10% discount if you sign up for the store rewards program. You give the cashier an email address. NeverBounce checks to see if the email is actually valid, and not something you just made up on the spot to get the discount.

NeverBounce is an incredibly useful piece of software for large corporations. If a sender tries to deliver an email to an invalid address, that action is a red flag, and the IP address the sender is using may come under scrutiny, which may lead to future emails ending up in the spam box. It's complicated; basically, just know that trying to deliver emails to invalid emails is a problem, and NeverBounce helps prevent that problem.

Brad has formed a mutually beneficial relationship between his company and MailChimp. MailChimp sends emails on behalf of businesses. If the email lists of businesses contain invalid emails, that hurts MailChimp. So, MailChimp promotes NeverBounce to all of its customers. Brad wins because he gains new customers, and MailChimp wins because any business using

NeverBounce has a much lower chance of trying to send emails to invalid addresses.

NeverBounce and MailChimp are two large companies, but you don't need a large company to form a mutually beneficial relationship. Consider the world of weddings. A wedding photographer could contact a cake decorator and agree to promote the other company to every new customer. People getting married need both cakes and photographs, so it works out well. Again, everyone wins.

The idea of mutualism is very powerful because whoever you partner with is already established. As such, your partner can send you a slew of customers in a split second, while still benefitting from the relationship. Everyone wins and you get customers.

Affiliates

There are two types of people in the world of internet marketing—vendors and affiliates. Vendors create products and may promote them as well. Affiliates do not own products—they simply promote the products of others for a cut of each sale. Utilizing affiliates is a good way to grow fast, as affiliates already know how to market products. If they choose to promote yours, you will get sales. Period.

Affiliates are fantastic. If you're in a space where you can use affiliates, you absolutely should. I can't imagine any reason why you wouldn't want to other than those people might, you know, promise things that can't deliver on but then again that's not your fault. And you can just manage those people. You could reach out to affiliates that they can or cannot say something. Affiliates are fantastic ways to move a company or software forward because they absorb all the marketing costs and as someone who does marketing, let me tell you that can get really expensive. They've got the audience already. I was speaking with a guy in my office, who's in the SEO space, who has a very popular blog and he recommends products and they're always affiliate products. His audience trusts him. So if I see a piece of software for sale I'm not gonna believe the company's promises but I will believe this guy, this influencer. I'll believe what he says and I'll take him at his word and I'll sign up. That value is really, really powerful and can't be bought. That level of trust with audiences can't just be bought overnight. It's worth big commissions to do it.

ILAN NASS

FOUNDER, TAKTICAL DIGITAL

Finding Affiliates

Sound too good to be true? Well, getting affiliates to promote your product is not as easy as it sounds. Affiliates with real influence are rare, and in a sense, you are competing with every other product owner out there for the attention of a small group of influential affiliates.

However, if you know what affiliates are looking for, you can still succeed in swaying them to promote your product. In fact, influential affiliates will often seek out good products to promote on their own. First and foremost, they will look for products with high EPCs (earnings per click). As in, how much money will the affiliate earn, on average, for every click he is able to send over to you? If your product costs $100, and your conversion rate is $2, and you give the affiliate a 50% cut of sales, then the EPC for him is $1.00. Depending on the industry, that may be a high or low EPC, but in general, know that the products with the highest EPCs are the ones that affiliates tend to promote. (There are other factors as well, like freshness of the product and how much it has been promoted within the industry already, but overall, EPC is the #1 metric that affiliates look at, by a longshot.)

To successfully find affiliates, raise your product's EPC. You can raise your EPC by doing things like creating a great product and making sure that you have great reviews for it. Overall, though, EPC is determined by how well your website converts visitors into sales. You can raise your conversion rate by split testing. For example, if you add a 60-second explanatory video, your conversion rate might double, which means your EPC would double, too. The product owner with the highest EPC gets the affiliates. Work on your website and your landing pages until you have a comparatively good EPC, then try to find affiliates. If your EPC is high, you will find that you have no trouble at all, but if it isn't, then you will struggle.

Measure the essentials. If I were the co-founder of a startup I'd be the one obsessed with numbers, making sure the essentials are tracked, making sure that we monitor ongoing performance (whether it's marketing, revenue, social media, etc.). Making sure you have robust measuring techniques from the onset is one of the keys to success for a startup.

BEN DONKOR

SOCIAL MEDIA ANALYST, MICROSOFT

The Commission You Offer

One of the major contributing factors to your EPC, aside from conversion rate, is the affiliate commission you offer (the percentage of the sale that the affiliate receives). Before you decide on the commission you will offer, you need to know your margins, or else you might put yourself out of business by accident. If you are selling an eBook you wrote yourself, then your margins are very high, and you can offer a sizeable commission. But if you are running a company like a car dealership, your margins are lower—perhaps you earn just $500 in profit from a $10,000 sale, which means you can't offer even 10% as a commission, or else you will lose money. In the software industry, you can usually offer a high commission, as the cost of adding new customers is quite low. Most of your costs are fixed in the development of the software, and the extra customer support needs of each new customer are negligible in the grand scheme of things. Offering 50% commission to affiliates is not unheard of, and actually quite common.

So, what commission rate do you offer? After you determine your margins, look to see what your competitors are offering. Unless you can beat their conversion rates in a significant way, you will usually have to offer something similar to what they are offering. If your commission rate is too low, your EPC will be low in turn, and affiliates will ignore you.

When you start looking around, you may find that some vendors are offering 100% affiliate commissions, which means they make a whopping

$0 per sale. This business model is made possible by upsells and downsells, which affiliates usually do not receive commissions for. If you offer 100% commissions, you will find it easier to find affiliates because your EPC will be very high, and even though you might make very little (or lose money) on affiliate commissions, you can still earn a pretty penny off upsells and downsells. (Upsells and downsells are collectively called OTOs (one-time offers) in the internet marketing industry).

There is a reason why the term "marketing funnel" exists. You can visualize the process of selling to customers as an actual funnel. The top of the funnel is the initial sale. From there, the funnel narrows, because only a percentage of customers will take you up on your first OTO. Even fewer will take you up on your second OTO, so the funnel narrows further. Now, you may offer all of your OTOs to all of your customers instead of presenting the next one only to customers who have purchased the previous one, and you may have two OTOs, or 10. Every marketing funnel is different. Building a highly-profitable funnel takes an extraordinary amount of marketing skill. You will need to learn this skill if you wish to compete for affiliates with other product owners who have.

CHAPTER 20

• • • • • • •

PRODUCT LAUNCHES

A product launch is the process of planning a product release date in advance, and recruiting affiliates before that date so they are all ready to push the product when it launches. As soon as the doors open, all your affiliates start pushing your product as soon as possible. With a set date and a bunch of affiliates ready to roll on that date, your first day or two of sales can easily be the biggest your company ever has. This strategy has its benefits, but also its consequences.

The benefits are fairly obvious. You make a ton of sales very quickly, which can help you recoup development costs almost immediately.

However, getting a lot of sales quickly does have its downsides. A year after your product launch, your product may be regarded as dead or stale to affiliates because it was pushed so heavily at the start. Growing pains are also very real. If your software has bugs in it, you will be flooded with support requests, and you may get a number of bad reviews right off the start, which can destroy your reputation as quickly as you can blink.

Product launches are cool. They give you a rush. And making many sales quickly is, of course, very appealing. But, if you are launching your first piece of software, I would recommend staying away from traditional product launches. You probably won't have everything perfect simply because you are a beginner, and the explosive growth can boomerang back in your face to ruin your long-term reputation.

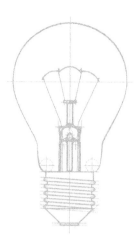

CHAPTER 21

• • • • • • • •

DIRECT SALES

veryone loves to hate on cold calling and cold emailing. But in the B2B space, there is no denying that it can work. You pick up the phone, compose the email, or even make the flight to do whatever you need in order to get in front of that big client. If you can deal with rejection, direct sales is something you may want to consider. I have had success with direct selling. Businesses can be awfully rude when you first reach out, but if you manage to cultivate interest and you remember to follow up, your close rate can be close to 100%. Seriously.

> *In the beginning, it's my recommendation and certainly many other business schools when you're starting, to sell direct. You're gonna fall down if you look at resellers immediately. So basically when selling to Central Texas College, this was a contact made through a convention where we would set up and we would meet some of the principals and follow-up and turn that into a paying client.*

JEFF MAYNARD

PRESIDENT AND CEO, BIOMETRIC SIGNATURE ID

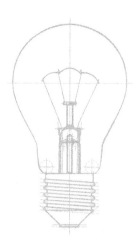

CHAPTER 22

• • • • • • • •

Grow Your Email List

When you have a product, you will find it easier to get email subscribers than if you didn't have one. You can give away a free complementary product to gather email addresses, or you can offer a free trial of your main product. What you send to email subscribers will depend on what your main product is. If your product promises results of some sort, you could send a case study detailing just how effective your product is. If your software provides a service, you could offer a free trial, because offering a free trial would probably cost you next to nothing. Regardless of how you get the email, once you do, you can send more info to that email and pitch your product in subsequent correspondences.

Here's a great example of a subsequent correspondence: I recently let my membership with LiveChat expire. LiveChat, as you can probably guess, provides live chat solutions for websites, and the company can help with sales tremendously, if your product is particularly complex or difficult to explain quickly. After I canceled, they sent an email with the subject line, "Would you ignore 696 people in your store?" During my free trial, 58 people had started live chats on my website, so they were asking me if I would let 696 people (58 people over the course of 12 months) go without help in my physical store. That email definitely made me think about buying the full LiveChat product.

StockX was the natural progression of a company called Campless, which we described as a 'sneakerhead data company.' It was, essentially, a price guide for sneakers. When we transitioned to a marketplace we already had an existing user base of sneakerheads using the price guide, so they quickly became both buyers and sellers.

JOSH LUBER

CO-FOUNDER, STOCKX

Email is the most valuable marketing channel for us. We have tended to avoid too many annoying pop ups on our blog to collect emails, mainly because our free plan has been a great source of subscribers. During our free trial we have a series of emails to aid conversions. We use actions in-app to trigger targeted messages as well as some targeting based on company size and role to keep things relevant. It's something we're constantly tweaking and improving, though. We then publish research on our blog that we think will be useful to subscribers and email that, though we don't email every single post.

JAMES BLACKWELL

CO-FOUNDER, BUZZSUMO

Well, initially, it was free. So that was really easy to get customers because it was free. We had like 50 or 60% signup conversion because like hey, why not give you my email and I get a free service? That's how we got 200,000 email addresses in what 9 months and those 200,000 email addresses added *up to like less than $2000 a month of revenue, but then we locked the doors on everybody and come to find out about 4000 or 5000 of those 200,000 actually valued us enough to pay for it so that's how we kind of got those. I'd say the way we got them was SEO. We did a lot of writing in the men's fashion niche. Men's fashion, in particular, was really easy to win on SEO. We wrote a ton of content. Made a bunch of videos, paid bloggers and thought-leaders to talk about us. And that worked, really well. Then switching to women, that game didn't work nearly as well for us, much more crowded marketplace. For that, we focused mostly on paid acquisition through Pinterest, which just killed for us as well as done a good bit on Facebook and Instagram. We used a couple influencers as well, and used a couple blogger influencers; specifically in the minimalism space, that kind of thing.*

BLAKE SMITH

CO-FOUNDER, CLADWELL

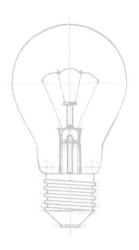

CHAPTER 23

• • • • • • • •

Pay-Per-Click Advertising

There are a whole lot of PPC networks on the market. Google and Facebook are by far the largest and most widely used, but Bing is also worth considering (it's like Google's little brother), and LinkedIn can help you reach business audiences in particular.

Google Adwords

Did you know? The vast majority of Google's revenue comes from selling ad space. You can buy ad space both on their search results and on webpages where webmasters are displaying Google ads (also known as display ads).

Search

When you bid on ads that are shown in the search results, you can appear at the top of Google for any keyword within any niche. Different niches command different rates. You can create a free Google Adwords account and play around with the Google Keyword Tool to check how much clicks will cost (on average) for any particular keyword.

The Google Keyword Tool just gives you an estimation, though. The actual process is slightly different. You specify the maximum you will pay for a click and Google will attempt to show your ad to people who cost less than your specified amount. There are dozens of factors that can affect how much a user click costs, but a big one is the country the user comes from. Countries like the US, UK, and Canada are all expensive, whereas countries like Bangladesh and Pakistan are quite cheap in comparison. A lower CPC (cost per click) is not always ideal, because users that cost more per click may convert at a higher rate.

Is your head spinning yet? Don't worry. There are a number of fantastic free tutorials on Google Adwords available for you to look at. Do some exploring if you are unfamiliar with Adwords. Below, we will cover a few strategies to lower your CPC while still maintaining high-quality traffic.

Start High, Finish Low

Start by setting your CPC at a value that is higher than what you actually want to spend. Once you start receiving traffic, lower it down to your desired amount. This strategy has allowed me to get a lower CPC than if I were to start immediately at my target CPC.

Test Different Ads

For every keyword you are bidding on, you should run a handful of different ads to see which one performs best. An ad that works for one keyword may not work for another. Every customer is looking for something different. A mother and an 18-year-old may be looking for the exact same product, but the same ads will not work for both of them, despite the fact that the product is identical to both.

Google will eventually give each of your ads a quality score from 1 to 10. Scrap your lowest-scoring ads and create variations of your highest-scoring ads. Even small variations can improve your quality score and slice your ad costs in half or more.

Maximize User Experience

If a user arrives at your website then clicks the back button, that user has "bounced." The percentage of users that bounce is referred to as your bounce rate. If your bounce rate is high, Google will increase your CPC for the keyword and/or ad because Google cares about giving its users a good experience. Make sure that your ads clearly explain what the user should expect in order to reduce your bounce rate and keep your CPC under control.

Use Ad Extensions

Here is a typical ad that you will see on Adwords. This typical ad has a title, URL, and two lines for the description. The ad is the first result for the keyword "tables". The word "tables" appears in both the title and the URL. The entire ad is just four lines long.

Economy Folding Tables - In Stock in Canada - uline.ca
[Ad] www.uline.ca/Folding-Tables ▾
ULINE - 35 Styles, Colors & Sizes in Stock! Same Day Shipping.
Fast Delivery · 32,500+ Products

For a more competitive search term like "hotels in Toronto," the top ad has what are known as ad extensions. One such extension is the 4.3 star rating. This extension is eye-catching and will improve CTR, which will in turn lower CPC. Along with the star rating, this ad also has two additional lines of text at the bottom of the ad, which makes the ad seven lines long in total. The ad with extensions has almost double the height of the ad without extensions, which means it is far more likely to catch the user's attention and result in a click.

Hotels in Toronto - booking.com
[Ad] www.booking.com/Toronto-Hotels ▾
4.7 ★★★★★ rating for booking.com
Lowest price guarantee! Book your **hotel in Toronto** Online.
24/7 Customer Service · Get Instant Confirmation · We speak your language · No Booking Fees
Ratings: Selection 10/10 - Fees 9.5/10 - Travel info 9.5/10 - Prices 9.5/10 - Service 9.5/10
Book for Tonight   Book Now

Use Keywords Throughout

As you can see in the ads above, the keyword appears in both the title and the URL. Lots of people use the keyword in the title, but not the URL, which is a mistake. Google's algorithm gives lower CPCs to the ads that mention the keyword in both the title and the URL. You don't even need to change your website's URLs to include the keyword, because the URL on the ad is the display URL, not the actual URL (you can set the display URL to anything you want but visitors will go to your actual URL when they click).

Find New Keywords

Adwords is tough to master as a new entrepreneur. But you don't need to reinvent the wheel. You can use tools like SEMRush and SpyFu to see what keywords your competitors are bidding on and what their ads for those keywords look like. From there, you can copy their strategies and often come up with winning campaigns without doing too much creative legwork yourself. Utilizing these spy tools is one of my favorite ways to grow a new business.

> *We don't do any PPC. We've actually done very little paid advertising. Part of the problem is we have struggled to find keywords that easily describe our product. We are not really in a traditional category in that sense e.g. "accounting software." People tend to find BuzzSumo via blog referrals, we also get a good bit of traffic from long tail SEO keywords through our blog.*
>
> **JAMES BLACKWELL**
> *CO-FOUNDER, BUZZSUMO*

Optimize for Mobile

Mobile has quickly become the norm. People are going to be using their phones to look at your product and to purchase it. At first, I didn't believe this fact, so I didn't optimize one of my software websites for mobile devices. The complaints quickly started rolling in and I almost certainly lost a few customers in the meantime. Do not underestimate the power of mobile. Mobile is huge and will only continue to grow.

Use Match Types

You can specify in Adwords how you want your keyword to be used when displaying ads to users. There are three types: broad, phrase, and exact. For example, if your keyword was "tables" and you selected the broad match type, you would tell Google that you wanted your ad displayed on any keyword that contained the word "tables" whatsoever. The table below can help you understand each match type more clearly.

	Tables	Hockey tickets	Tractors
Broad	Tables, kitchen tables, coffee tables, counter tops, desks, etc	Hockey tickets, hockey tickets for sale, NHL tickets, AHL tickets, etc	Tractors, John Deere tractors, compact utility tractor, backhoe, combine, etc
"Phrase"	Tables, kitchen tables, coffee tables, etc	Hockey tickets, hockey tickets for sale, etc	Tractors, John Deere tractors, compact utility tractor, etc
[Exact]	Tables	Hockey tickets	Tractors

Check Your Adwords Account Every Day

Google will take your money even if your ads are not performing. It is your responsibility to make sure they are performing well. Spend at least 5-10 minutes every day analyzing your ad performance and making changes. Ads that are not performing should be canned, and ads that are performing should be amplified and replicated.

Try Bing Ads

Bing Ads is identical to Google Adwords in many ways. If you find success on Adwords, you should consider moving the campaign over to Bing

Ads as well, as you will be able to get more profitable traffic, and possibly even a cheaper CPC.

Display

Display ads are different from search ads. They are displayed inside a website instead of on Google's search results. You may have seen ads with "AdChoices" in fine print at the bottom of them. Those are display ads from Adwords.

Display ads have some good aspects to them. You can generally get cheaper clicks. You can use images. And you can expand your reach, because instead of relying just on Google traffic, you can access Google's entire publisher base, which is enormous.

But display ads also have their drawbacks. One major drawback is fraud. Webmasters click on their own ads to get paid, which means you are charged for a click, but the "visitor" is useless and will never make a purchase. Now, Google does have one of the most advanced anti-fraud systems in the industry, but fraud does still slip through. I have friends who spend thousands of dollars on Adwords ads every single day, and they never use display ads at all. You don't have to use them. I do use display ads, because I have found success with them if I have some safeguards in place. Those safeguards are explained below.

Target by Domain

Instead of finding websites to display your ad on via keyword, you can just enter the domain names you want to display ads on directly. Adwords has an internal search engine you can use to find websites to display ads on, or you can find industry sites that display Adsense (the publisher version of Adwords) and use those. This domain-only strategy lets you access the display network without the risk of displaying ads on garbage and possibly-fraudulent websites.

Retargeting

Have you ever gone to a website, failed to make a purchase, then seen ads for that website magically appear everywhere you go? That process is called retargeting. You can install a Google tracking pixel on your website that will take note of every visitor who lands on it. Then, you may create ads that target only previous visitors to your website! Retargeting is a fantastic way to capitalize on Google's display network, and since the CPC from retargeting is usually about the same as with your regular ads, retargeting is something that you should seriously consider implementing if you decide to use the display network.

Facebook

Facebook has its own ad network (which also allows you to advertise on Instagram). Other social networks have their own ad networks, too. Even though social ads and search/display ads are different mediums, they both have a surprising amount of similarities. We'll cover a few of my tips for Facebook ads below.

Advertise to Your Email List

Once you have an email list, you can import that list into Facebook and advertise to everyone who has an email on the list linked to a Facebook account. You can certainly advertise to your own email list... but Facebook does not verify that you own the email list you are advertising to, which means you can advertise to any random list of email addresses you can find. Perhaps you scrape emails from another website and import them into Facebook. The opportunities are endless; you just have to be creative.

Retargeting

Retargeting on Facebook is cheaper than it is on Adwords. And, Facebook is slightly better for retargeting than Adwords is, because people on Facebook probably have nothing better to do than look at your product. Even a daily budget of $1 can bring a pretty significant number of people back to your website who lost interest in it beforehand, whereas that same ad spend on Adwords would yield significantly fewer return visitors.

Video Ads

The best part about Facebook and Instagram is that both platforms give you the ability to use videos in your ad. Image and text ads can work, but they only go so far. Yes, you can buy video ads on YouTube through Adwords, but the reach isn't nearly as good as it is with Facebook/Instagram, and the rules for YouTube ads are stricter. With a solid personal video advertisement that is set to retarget customers, you can generate a huge chunk of extra revenue every month with relatively little ad spend.

Lookalike Audiences

You might find success with an audience on Facebook, but if the audience you find success with is small, you will burn through your campaign fairly quickly. To go further with a successful campaign, you can use the Lookalike Audience feature from Facebook, which is when Facebook takes your successful audience and tries to find others who fit the same characteristics. For example, if you run an ad targeted at the people who watched at least 50% of your first ad, once you show the ad to those people, you can choose to serve the same ad to a lookalike audience. Even though the lookalike audience didn't watch your first video ad, these people may still work for your campaign, because they share similar characteristics to the people who did watch the ad.

Text Ratio

Adding text to your images adds extra clarification to your ad, which may cause it to catch attention at a higher rate, which may increase your CTR. Not all successful ad images contain text, but many do. You should split test to determine if you can increase your CTR by adding text to your images. Keep in mind that Facebook requires your image to be made up of less than 20% text.

When it comes to finding your sales channel, there's no substitute for research. And you've gotta be heavily involved in research from the get-go, and in my opinion you've gotta have a team that is both marketing, sales, and technology driven. You have to have both components of that. And, yes, initially I would go to various universities and or set up meeting times with experts and I would solicit their input for help in terms of just helping establish my thoughts or my directions that I wish to go and see what they could help me validate that. Initially, I had some help with people who were involved in biometrics, who you have to participate in whatever sector you're developing in and you've got to either take the time to visit personally or at conferences, when such occur, to validate your assumptions.

JEFF MAYNARD

PRESIDENT AND CEO, BIOMETRIC SIGNATURE ID

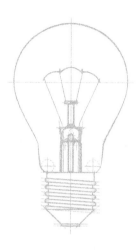

CHAPTER 24

• • • • • • • •

SOCIAL MEDIA

A s soon as you register your domain name, you should register a few of the top social media profiles for your company, too. Start with Facebook and Twitter. You will be running ads through your Facebook profile. Claim your URL and add your logo as your profile picture along with some sort of cover photo. Do the same on Twitter. Though you might not run ads on Twitter, users will naturally go to your Twitter if your website is down, so you should make sure you are available on the platform if that does happen. You may also consider registering a YouTube profile and adding a short video explaining your product. Even a couple hundred organic views on that video can result in extra sales every month.

B2C companies should register profiles on a few other social networks, too, namely Pinterest, Instagram, and Tumblr. These platforms can help you connect with your consumer audiences. If you are a B2B company, you can safely ignore these consumer-oriented social platforms.

Generally, video always performs best, regardless of platform. In terms of other media, anything "powerful" does well, and we also try to elicit an emotional response with our social copy. It's hard to gauge, but if a user "feels something" after consuming our content, the post is a success.

SCOTT WARD
SOCIAL MEDIA COORDINATOR, DENVER BRONCOS

YouTube in particular serves another purpose: managing your reputation in search engines. You can purchase $6 videos on Fiverr from amateur actors who will talk about your products. Then, you can upload those videos to YouTube with titles like "[YourProduct] [Year] Review." Google loves YouTube, so the positive videos will usually rank high up without any extra effort from you. Make sure the reviews aren't fake or untruthful, as that is against FTC guidelines. Label them as reviews, but the content within should be more of a tutorial than a review.

If you fail to take the initiative on targeting review keywords, unhappy customers may beat you to the punch, and all of your reviews will be negative, even if customers love your product overall. Your unhappy customers are always the loudest and your happy customers rarely speak up. I learned that lesson from one of my mentors, Don, after I noticed all of my review keywords had negative results ranking high up, even though customers generally liked my product. You can also incentivize your happy customers to share their thoughts with the world in exchange for discounts or other perks.

PR probably plays too much of a role for many tech companies and startups and not enough of a role for others. On the too much side, there are many startups who spin a story via media attention, become media darlings and later can't nearly live up to that role. The media loves a good success story, but not as much as a good demise story. It sets unrealistic expectations for the founders, their team, their investors and often goes bust.

For other companies, they don't leverage a media presence at all, and so they don't become known by potential investors, potential customers, potential employees or potential collaborators. With social media allowing companies to control their own messaging, there's really little excuse for not having some level of "media relations," unless, of course, you want to be stealth by design.

CAROL ROTH

TV CONTRIBUTOR AND BEST-SELLING AUTHOR

I still, today, remember our first ever customer of the Screaming Frog SEO Spider. It was Branko Rihtman (@neyne), who is a great guy I had chatted with on Twitter. I didn't know him personally, but we had exchanged a few tweets chatting about SEO stuff. We didn't target him in particular, we simply built our software and then released it. I wrote a blog post and tweeted about it. I was, and am still, quite active socially within the SEO community, sharing experiments, and chatting about the industry, etc. So, when we released the tool (which is free, and paid), some of my friends and followers trialed the software, found it useful and bought it. After that, it just slowly built up as more people used the tool, told others, wrote blog posts, spoke about it at conferences, etc.

It's easy when you understand your audience and already part of the community. We just solved a problem that we (as an SEO agency) were experiencing, and knew others were as well.

DAN SHARP

FOUNDER, SCREAMING FROG

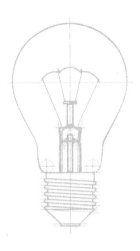

CHAPTER 25

• • • • • • • •

REPUTATION

B uying something online is risky. Buyers are worried about outright scams and misrepresented products. They will often do research on software and the creator of the software before committing to a purchase.

The same goes for any type of product. Take designer sunglasses as an example. I was recently shopping for a new pair of shades, and because I understand that designer sunglasses are often marked up exorbitantly, I started looking at overseas sellers offering half the price or less on domestic retailers. The issue with buying overseas is that scams are in abundance and more often than not you will end up buying a replica if you're not careful. So, I turned to forums, mainly Reddit, to find a reliable overseas seller. The one I was considering ended up being a scam. I was referred to another seller, who I ended up choosing, and I received a legit (and affordable) pair of designer sunglasses. If a product or company is used and liked by those in the industry (in my case, people who really like designer sunglasses), that means a whole lot, and can influence buyer decisions greatly, as it did for me.

Reputation is everything. A great tactic is to find a well-known company who might engage with you if you give them access to your product and service for free. Free can often overcome reputational issues and then it gives you a reference point for future buyers. It's always great to be able to say "XX Big Company" is a client of ours. That also overcomes you being small and establishes credibility.

I would also say that you should make sure the business and its key employees are presented well online. If a potential partner or customer does a search and questionable personal content is all that they can find, that doesn't bode well for your relationship.

CAROL ROTH

TV CONTRIBUTOR AND BEST-SELLING AUTHOR

Monitor Your Reputation

You can control your reputation by monitoring keywords related to your brand name, as most product research is done through Google. Basically, you search for your brand name and product name with "scam," "review," and other key phrases attached at the end.

If you find a negative review, you should first validate that the review is from an actual customer. If the review is legit, do everything in your power to contact the customer and rectify the situation. If you can make the customer happy, he will usually be more than happy to take down the negative review.

There will be some cases when the review is not from a valid customer, and a competitor is trying to ruin your good name to drive customers away from you and towards himself. If this situation occurs, first try contacting the web host to get the content removed. If that attempt fails, contact a lawyer, and he will be able to point you in the right direction.

These methods of monitoring your reputation can work, but they are sometimes futile, and the bad review stays up. You can get ahead of invalid negative reviews by filling up the Google search results for review-related keywords ahead of time. One way to fill up the search results, aside from review videos you generate yourself, is with software review directories. You list your software in a number of directories, and because these directories hold authority in the eyes of Google, the review pages start ranking right away. At the start, the pages might be empty (no reviews), but that is better than a bad review. If you get bad reviews on directories, you sometimes have the option to respond to them, which can negate the bad review in the eyes of a potential customer if you respond correctly. Finally, these software review directories can outrank existing bad reviews, so even if you already have a poor reputation, try this approach.

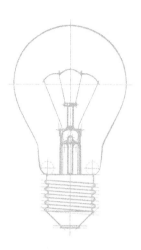

CHAPTER 26

• • • • • • •

WORD-OF-MOUTH

Word-of-mouth is powerful, especially in the digital world. Every industry is made up of people, and between the people in an industry exists an underlying web of connections. If you can push your product into this web, you can create a serious edge for yourself, and close many sales that you wouldn't otherwise.

Most beginners bounce from one industry to another and never really make a name for themselves. As such, they never access the underlying web in any single industry. I like to build a product and stick with it for 12+ months so that everyone I know in the industry becomes aware of it, and tells their friends in turn. However, this approach only goes so far, as you will have limited friends within each industry you wish to break into. Your customers will be the main source of word-of-mouth. You get your customers talking by making them not just happy, but exceptionally happy. You have to knock their socks off if you want them to do your promotion for you. You don't have to (products can succeed without sales driven by word-of-mouth), but never forget the potential of accessing that elusive underlying web of connections.

> *The biggest percentage of customers that we get are either word of mouth or being a byproduct of using the product. So, if someone attends a webinar and thinks it's awesome then they'll sign up for a demo on our site. There's a little bit of a viral aspect and that's really nice, and that's why we focus so much on creating a great product because it markets itself.*
>
> **WYATT JOZWOWSKI**
> *CO-FOUNDER, DEMIO*

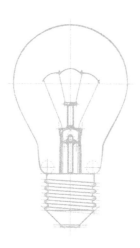

CHAPTER 27

• • • • • • •

INBOUND MARKETING

O utbound marketing is when you try to push your product onto people regardless of whether they want to hear about it or not. Television and radio ads are both examples of outbound marketing. Outbound marketing can still work, but it is being replaced by inbound marketing, which is far more effective and affordable for the vast majority of businesses.

Inbound marketing is when you pull customers to you by offering something they want for free, then trying to convert them into paying customers. For example, I have a company that helps companies grow their Instagram followings called Shout Our Biz. If I wanted to utilize inbound marketing, I could write a blog post explaining 5 to 10 ways to gain more followers, then rank it in Google. When a potential customer arrived at the blog post, he would gain valuable insight, but I would still have the opportunity to plug my service at the end of the post.

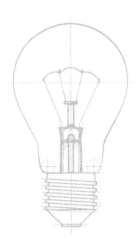

CHAPTER 28

• • • • • • • •

Search Engine Optimization

have mentioned SEO a few times beforehand, but not the specifics. We're going to cover the specifics now. I have been involved with SEO since 2009, and I know a whole lot about it. The entire process is very complicated, but even if you know the just the basics below, you will be able to position yourself competitively.

Write Awesome Free Content

Google ranks your website based on which words you mention within your content. If you don't know SEO, you probably think that means you should stuff your content full of a bunch of keywords. Don't do that. Instead, focus on writing valuable information that people will get real value out of. Don't try to fool Google unless you know exactly what you are doing.

Get Mentioned

If you can get mentioned on other websites, Google will be more likely to rank you high in the search engine results. Every website has a different value in the eyes of Google. For example, a mention in an article of a local newspaper holds quite a bit of weight, whereas a blog comment on an unrelated website does not. A popular strategy is writing blog posts for smaller websites (called guest posts) and slowly working your way up to larger websites. When you write a guest post, your "payment" from the other website is usually a link back to your website.

Give Your Users a Good Experience

User experience consists of things like website loading speed, design quality, and user satisfaction (whether the user finds what he needs or not). You want the user to have a good time on your website. If any part of your website is lackluster (like if your design looks like it is from 2002), then users won't spend as much time on your website, and Google will notice.

Hire an Agency

Create valuable content and get links: that's the foundation of SEO. SEO is always changing, so if I included anything past the foundation, the information would likely be outdated in a couple of years. You have two options if you wish to go further with SEO. You can hire an agency, either locally or remotely, to handle your SEO work. If you choose this route, make sure to research the agency fully, because there are heaps of scammers in the SEO space. You can also do more research and do everything yourself. If you choose this route, you can check out my website and my YouTube channel to learn quite a bit. There are other great resources, too—just look around.

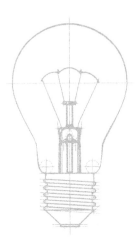

CHAPTER 29

• • • • • • • •

FREE AND TRIAL VERSIONS

ree and trial versions open your software up to a larger audience, which has the potential to help or harm your brand.

Demio has a strange path. We built it out over a year and we started bringing in customers on a paid beta through manual outreach to people we knew that had the same problem. We initially had up to $2500 in monthly recurring revenue, it was nothing crazy but that's when we realized we weren't happy with the technical foundation as it was still based on the original agency that we hired. So we decided to close beta at that time, which was really scary to do because we were just starting to get revenue, we invested too much money and we had constant expenses going out. We closed it and completely rebuilt the architecture and then came back to launch an MVP as a free beta and put that out there, ran some ads. A lot of people were sharing it because it was totally free to use during beta. We had about 900 or 1000 beta members

*and then we converted it after 3 or 4 months of beta to paid. I think 50 or
60 of the beta members converted into paying customers.*

WYATT JOZWOWSKI

CO-FOUNDER, DEMIO

Freemium

Free versions attract freeloaders. Freeloaders are generally pretty
social people, and they will tell others about their experiences with your
product, whether those experiences are good or bad. With a solid product,
this socializing can benefit you. But if your software has a bunch of bugs or
doesn't work quite right, freeloaders can destroy your brand before you can
establish a foothold.

The goal with a free version is to provide enough value so that users
incorporate the software into their routines… but not so much value that they
will see no point in upgrading. You have to strike a perfect balance. You can
look at other freemium software to see what they offer and don't offer in their
free versions in order to get ideas for your own freemium software.

*Only if the free version and the paid version have enough of a difference to
convert. If you have a free version that I don't need the paid, or you have to
come up with excuses that I have to pay, then you're gonna fail. Evernote is
an example of this where their free product is so good that there's no reason to
pay and very few people do. Whereas, you know there's a lot of other products
where the free version is really nothing more than a shitty demo. I'm an
advocate of 'you can have a free version but it really shouldn't be very good.'
Buffer is an example of a company that has a free version that is fine if you
want to like schedule a few things here and there, or if you just wanna play
with it. But once you start buffering more and more, and get to rely on it, it's
not enough. And I started paying. Because you just cannot live on 10 buffers.
You just can't. I'm scheduling like 30 buffers in a row it's insane that I have
to stop at ten. I kept banging into this limit and it kept driving me crazy.*

ILAN NASS

FOUNDER, TAKTICAL DIGITAL

Trials

Offering a trial version of your software allows you to prove to customers that your software can indeed do everything it promises. Trial versions do not necessarily help with growth, but they do improve conversion rates. People will be more likely to give your software a try, and if they like what they see, they will purchase once the trial is over. Some developers believe that offering a trial version cheapens the brand; you will have to decide if the tradeoff is worth it.

You can offer a free trial, or, you can offer an inexpensive paid trial. If your software costs $97 per month, you might charge $0 for the trial, or you might charge $1 to validate interest. Either works. A completely free trial might get more downloads, but a paid trial might result in more trial users converting into paid subscribers.

> *For us, it took quite long [to get our first customer], purely because we started with a public beta. It was 9 months after running the beta, which was incredibly successful, but we were literally so worried if anyone wanted to give us any money at this point. I remember we switched off the beta. We had prepared really well for this. We gave one month for free. We allowed our users make the choice or downgrade to a free simpler version of Hotjar. And then, yeah, in all this nerve-wracking moment we saw our first customer pop up and it was Homes.com.*
>
> **DR. DAVID DARMANIN**
> *CO-FOUNDER, HOTJAR*

Some people do free trials for a period of time but the key that I've found is there's something called a hook point. There's a moment in time when someone, who is using a piece of software or an app, truly feels it's value for a moment, they really like it. You have to make sure that your trial goes right up to that point and no further. And that's really tough to do but that's the idea.

ILAN NASS

FOUNDER, TAKTICAL DIGITAL

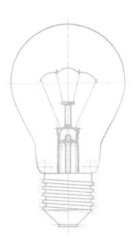

CHAPTER 30

• • • • • • • •

IDENTIFY YOUR CUSTOMER

So many entrepreneurs who build products fail to thoroughly consider who the best customers for the product will be. Imagine you own a Ford car dealership and you are trying to offload 15 Ford transit vans to make room for next year's model. You could sell these vans by taking out an ad in the local newspaper, and you might succeed in selling them all to regular consumers. But if you were to reconsider who your ideal customer is, you might decide that selling them all in one go to a local telecommunications provider would be the better route. Both methods of selling the vans can work, but one might be more effective than the other. In both cases, you are selling the exact same product, but by clearly thinking about your ideal customer and the sales process behind reaching your customer, you can make a better business decision.

Since the app was currently geared for men, we were maybe getting 10 or 15 emails a week from women saying, "would you build this for us?" and that *was kind of a big turning point for us. Where suddenly I asked the question. "If we had built this thing for women, I wonder if men would be emailing me you know 10 or 15 times a week asking me to build this for them." I was like, I kind of doubt it. I wonder if we're fishing on the wrong side of the boat. So we slapped together a test and tried it out for women and it popped. We went from making around $15,000 a month to like over $1,000,000 a year, in less than a year.*

BLAKE SMITH

CO-FOUNDER, CLADWELL

I think there's the issue of special product market fit, and trying to find where you belong and what your technology or your product is best used for is a huge challenge. Probably the biggest challenge after building a product is finding out who exactly is going to make the most use of it. And from what I've seen, it doesn't really grow beyond trial and error. It doesn't move past that. Or talking to your users and isolating heavy users and finding out what they're about. But you see if you get that first batch of users in the door and you'll see—you'll see the difference in patterns. I'm sure Unbounce, for example, made these decision or discovered these things because maybe they had 500 companies on their platform but 3 companies or 10 companies were heavy users while the others maybe used the free product and then didn't log in all the time or something like that, but the other guys were logging in 3 times a day. And they did this by analyzing the data of their users. They did this by talking to their users, emailing them, and interacting with people. And you know, for example Unbounce might recognize that agencies like mine are some of their biggest customers because we're the ones that bring the other customers in. Which we do, I mean I personally have given Unbounce 20-25 paying customers because as an agency I introduce my clients to the concept of it. I teach them what they need to know and I kind of resell it for them. And so they might discover that agencies are great, or they might discover that larger companies are great. They might discover that e-commerce companies are really great. And the only way to do that is really examine the data.

ILAN NASS

FOUNDER, TAKTICAL DIGITAL

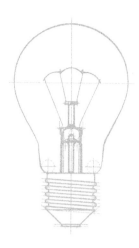

CHAPTER 31

• • • • • • • •

REVERSE THE BUYER PROCESS

To market your product in the most effective way, you must realize how the typical buyer would go about finding a product like yours. If the product is the first of its kind, people would not be searching Google for it, so SEO would not work well for you. Instead, you would probably need to create an explanatory video and advertise that video on different websites, like Facebook.

Every product has a different buyer process. If you sell something to car dealerships, maybe you need to work your way into magazines made for car dealerships. If you sell marketing tools, maybe you have to pick up the phone, call marketing agencies, and attempt to demo your product for them. If you sell antivirus software, maybe you have to appear in publications that rank the best antivirus software products of the year for consumers. If you sell photo editing software, maybe you create connections with website owners who review popular alternatives to the big names in photo editing, like

Photoshop. If you sell software for elementary schools, maybe you need to start networking and befriending a key decision-maker somewhere…

You get the point. Every piece of software will have a different ideal sales method. Put yourself in the shoes of your buyer and think about how a buyer like that would find the type of software you are creating, then be present wherever that is.

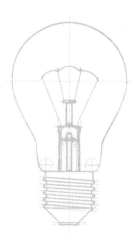

CHAPTER 32

• • • • • • • •

MEDIA APPEARANCES

At a certain point you will want to start hunting down media appearances. Everything from podcasts to blogs to television should be considered.

Guest Posts

Last year I had the opportunity to ask the CEO of SEMRush a question (he was holding an ask-me-anything in a private marketing group that I am a member of). SEMRush is a well-known SEO tool and they have been around forever. But I was more interested in their roots. So I asked the CEO what made the software take off at the start. He answered my question and told me that it was most likely due to a mention on a blog called SEOBook, almost a decade ago.

In many industries, bloggers wield immense power, just as the media does when it comes to politics. Your job is to find the influential bloggers and reach out to them. If you can get yourself onto one of these influential blogs, a few thousand blog readers might result in more sales than a few hundred thousand generic ad views would.

So, how do you get on a blog, aside from reaching out and asking? Sometimes, you can write a guest post for the blog that mentions your brand in some way. If the post is good and the blog is a smaller one, you may get published for free. Larger blogs will almost always have a dedicated in-house writer, so if this is the case, you can try to offer your insight on a particular piece in exchange for some publicity. Lastly, you can buy native advertising on many publications. Native advertising is when the publication publishes your promotional story in exchange for a fee. The story will be marked as sponsored in most cases, but most people don't notice, so you are essentially buying an organic guest post for your company.

Help a Reporter Out

When reporters need to find an interviewee for a story, they may use a website called Help A Reporter Out. You can sign up to Help A Reporter Out and you will receive scheduled emails with opportunities for media appearances. Most won't fit your company, but if the opportunity seems like a good fit, you can contact the reporter directly, and possibly get featured in whatever publication the reporter writes for. You won't always hear back from the reporter (even if you think you are a perfect fit), but I have used Help A Reporter Out with success in the past to land appearances that I would not have gotten otherwise.

My success rate has probably been about 30-40% of the ones that I'll respond to. And I've definitely been doing a lot of testing around it to get better responses. I used to write like big, long responses and makes you realize you're basically doing cold outreach when the goal is to get a response. So, what I'll do is respond, I'll give them a couple sentences about myself and actually, I responded to one yesterday, for example, that was for TechCrunch and gave them enough to kind of whet their whistle and say you know they were asking for entrepreneur stories and the challenges of building a business. I gave them six points on all the challenges I've been through: losing 60% of my customers in 10 days because of a software bug, being personally depressed there for a while and working with a therapist, rebranding and pivoting my business model within a couple months. I gave them those sorts of things and then really saying if you think this is pertinent to what you're looking for, I'd love to talk about it further. I found that to work better and some just people won't get back to you. I responded to one about, I'm an ENTJ in the Meyer's Briggs, so what like Napoleon and Steve Jobs and people like that. I responded to someone asking for the challenges that ENTJs have working remotely. I responded to it. I never heard back and then two weeks later I get notified on LinkedIn that she included what I said in her article. Right so, sometimes you're not going to get a response but you're going to get a mention.

JOHN DOHERTY

FOUNDER, CREDO

Television

I've never been on TV, but I had the distinct privilege to speak with Carol Roth, who has appeared on (almost) every TV station in the country. Take it away, Carol.

I would ask a startup founder why they would want to be on TV? Their answer should inform their steps. The reality is that there are not a lot of business programs that host start-up founders in the strict TV medium, unless they are one of the chosen few/unicorns. The reason to go on business TV would be if they are planning to go public or be acquired and want to gain some credibility within the investor community or with large company CEOs. If their desire is to get customer attention, then the question is, "where do my target consumers go for information on TV where my appearance would be relevant?" If you sell a product geared at busy moms, maybe a morning show would have you, but again, there aren't a lot of slots to get on TV.

If you want to get on TV, the best way is to do something stupid. As they say in the business, "if it bleeds, it leads." Otherwise, do something clever and build up relationships. Start small, too; it's much easier to get on the local news as a hot startup in the area than to try for a national appearance.

And by god, if you do land a TV appearance, practice before you go. Sit in front of any video camera- even on your phone- and practice answering questions. TV is a medium of short "sound-bites," so practice giving enough but not too much information. Watch previous episodes of the show to see how the host conducts interviews and make sure that you understand their cues, like when they are trying to interrupt to end the segment. Know specifically what message you want to get across and if the outlet will allow you to plug a site. And then, finally, dress well. No white, stripes or tight patterns that will make the camera go bonkers—that won't be appreciated by anyone.

Finally, I would suggest that founders look past TV to other media. Media is holistic these days. Look to podcasts, webcasts, blogs, online articles, social media, and more places to get out messaging and establish expertise.

CAROL ROTH

TV CONTRIBUTOR AND BEST-SELLING AUTHOR

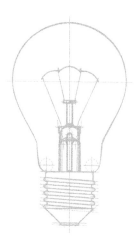

CHAPTER 33

• • • • • • • •

INFLUENCER MARKETING

Consumer markets are led by influences, who are popular figures within any industry. For example, in the fitness industry, there are many fitness guru influencers on Instagram with thousands or millions of followers. If you were launching a new protein powder, you may attempt to get these fitness guru influencers to promote your product via an Instagram post. With this strategy, you can reach consumers who are perfect fits for your product, and your product is promoted by someone with a respected name, which is usually superior traditional advertising methods.

To find an influencer for your product, you can research the top ones in your market, contact them (or their agencies), and get pricing for a post. To streamline this process, you may want to check out a piece of software called Shout Our Biz (owned by yours truly). With Shout Our Biz, you can browse influencers by niche, compare them, and reach out to the ones you find interesting with the email addresses provided on the platform.

If we were starting over, we might be smarter in how we invite 'influencers' in the SEO community to trial our software (so they speak about it at conferences and events) to raise awareness quicker.

DAN SHARP

FOUNDER, SCREAMING FROG

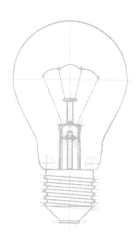

CHAPTER 34

• • • • • • •

FORTUNE 500 COMPANIES

ortune 500 companies are fascinating to me because of the extra layer of contracts within any agreement. If you sign a deal with Coca-Cola, you're going to have to lay out all of the specifics of your product ahead of time… but if you can get the contract signed, that deal may be worth what 100 regular customers are worth, or more.

Though I haven't yet signed a contract with a Fortune 500 company directly, I do have some experience selling to them indirectly. For example, I closed a software deal with the agency that manages Victoria's Secret. I'll tell you how I made these larger deals, then let my contributors give you their thoughts on dealing with the corporations directly.

You can reach Fortune 500 companies through traditional B2B outreach, like cold calling and cold emailing. But you need to put extra effort into every outreach you do. You need to reach the right people with the perfect message. Nothing less will cut it. Build a list yourself—don't buy anything—then tailor a specific message to each individual contact on the list. Generic messages don't work. Can you imagine how many emails and phone calls these people get? You have to really stand out if you want them to take notice of you.

Another way to get noticed is by speaking at relevant industry events and conferences. Fortune 500 companies will usually send a representative to see what's going on. If you can land a speaking position somewhere, you will get an immediate opportunity to land a Fortune 500 client, along with any other potential client who happens to attend.

Also keep in mind that decision-makers at Fortune 500 companies do the same type of research when choosing new products and services as other businesses do. If a Fortune 500 company needs a piece of software to solve a particular problem, the purchasing department will go through a series of steps, including comparing alternatives and requesting demos/quotes. If your software is included wherever they are looking, and you have elements on your landing page to cater to enterprise clients, you may receive outreach from a Fortune 500 company just like that. (From there, you will have to convince the Fortune 500 company your software and your company can handle a client of that magnitude, among other things.)

It's very different because they have a lot more money and they're very, very structured. The way I found my first Fortune 500 client is the way you find anything within the world and the client-services world that I live in, which is mainly based on referrals. I went to meet this Fortune 500 company based on referral. I walked up and they did not have a conference room booked for us because they were so busy so I sat in their lobby in New York before security on their couch and I pitched to them without a deck and later that day they gave us a contract. It was a very informal way to begin but once working them it's obviously a heavily-structured global company. It was a very different way to work with a client.

ADAM CUNNINGHAM
FOUNDER, 87AM

It is slower [selling to Fortune 500s]. We usually see it's around 5-6 months of asking questions back and forth but we're very focused on the self-service model but it's kind of an assisted self-service model so we do help them out by sharing information that they need but anything we do quite repetitively then we think how do we self-service it. Having said that, we feel very comfortable saying to a big company "No," when we feel they're trying to break too much out of the model. We have a strategic plan, like when taking on a big client and they want to change the product or impact that then we obviously politely say "no," and even tell them who they should probably go to instead. But if it is a big enterprise or a Fortune 500 but they are agile in the way they work and reasonable and happy with self-service model for us it makes no difference. We just try and avoid working with firms that lets say are a little bit too traditional in their approach and expect software companies to change the software to suit specifically them.

DR. DAVID DARMANIN

CO-FOUNDER, HOTJAR

BONUS

. . . .

Cashing Out

You may come to a point where you have a successful software company, but you're just sick of it. You're done. You know it's profitable but you want to try something different. If this is the case, you may decide to sell your company. Or, you may decide that it's worth it if you can grow significantly faster, and you may want to raise capital from outside sources.

Selling Your Company

When you try to sell your software company, you have two options. You can try to sell the company yourself, or you can hire a broker. It's entirely possible to sell it yourself, and if you manage to, you keep all of the money for yourself (aside from escrow fees). But, you may not know the right buyers who will pay you the maximum amount possible. With a broker, you pay a commission to the broker (which is sometimes quite substantial), but the broker is often able to fetch a much higher price for your company due to having connections that you do not have.

Imagine you have a company that nets $10,000 in profit every month. You have been growing steadily over the past 18 to 24 months and you believe that now is the perfect time to cash out. If you sell by yourself, you may be able to fetch an 18x valuation, or $180,000. Not bad at all. But a broker would be able to fetch a much higher valuation, possibly 30x instead of 18x. With a broker, your company would sell for $300,000 instead of $180,000, and even if the broker took a 20% cut ($60,000), you would still bring home $60,000 more than if you sold your company yourself ($240,000 instead of $180,000). This situation isn't always the case; sometimes, the broker might not be able to fetch a significantly higher valuation, and you are better off selling the company yourself.

Overall, the multiple of monthly profit that you or a broker can demand is based on a large number of factors, including but not limited to type of business, financial trends, age of the business, stability of the business, and how much room there is to expand.

When building a company to sell, realize revenue diversity and client acquisition strategies are metrics buyers tend to focus on because they want to know how you previously on-boarded paying customers and how stable the company's revenue is. Human resources alone are an asset. Be prepared, it's common for purchasers to want top level executives and partner companies to contractually agree to continue once the ownership transition is complete.

JOSEPH MONGAN

RECENTLY SOLD HIS INTERNET COMPANY THROUGH A BROKER

Raising Capital

Growing pains are very real. If your company grows quickly, you may find that you have adequate cash flow to cover your costs of growing, which is when you would seek extra capital from an outside source. I have never had to seek outside capital, but then again, I have never founded a billion-dollar startup. Maybe you will.

We ended up with 4 investors in the A round. I just went and talked to people, I had some introductions as well, but remember I was a successful entrepreneur now. Bluefin has been a big success and we started a venture that made money and was sold. If you say, "hey I made this successful venture and I made a lot of money for everybody and I want to do another one"— it's an easy conversation. We had put together a very impression team, 10 people who said they wanted to join that was composed of top academics, top engineers from industry, a lot of experience and bunch of young talented guys, a really nice mix. We didn't have a lot in presentation material but we had a fantastic team and a great track record.

FRANK VAN MIERLO
FOUNDER, 1366 TECHNOLOGIES

When seeking investors, focus on your strengths and hand-pick potential investors who have already invested in similar startups within similar niches. Venture capitalists are known to scoop up companies so they can dominate a particular industry before investing in startups within that same industry. If you go to the website of a venture capitalist, you will see startups sorted by category. If you see a category that your software fits into, then that venture capitalist may be interested in your product. If you don't, the venture capitalist probably won't even consider investing in you, so move your efforts elsewhere.

It's rare that we invest in a founder regardless of product and idea or product and market, although I've done it before based on it being a cool founder, who's got an idea and it's like, okay, I don't this idea is gonna work but I know this guy's gonna figure it out, so it does happen, it's unusual. Generally, we invest in our market. So, if I think AI is gonna be big, I'm looking for AI companies. If I think fintech is gonna be big I'm looking for fintech companies.

We at 500 Startups really focus on diversity. So a typical venture fund averages about 6% female co-founders, the number of minorities is vanishingly small.

For us it's about 30% female and it's something that we're pretty proud of and you know, go to lengths to make sure we find good non-traditional founders.

SANJAY SINGHAL

CANADIAN VENTURE PARTNER, 500 STARTUPS

Once you find a venture capitalist that seems to be a good fit, how on earth do you get the ball rolling? Some will accept unsolicited pitches, and some won't accept any at all. Due to this fact, you will find it useful to create a personal brand for yourself early on. I have spent countless hours building up a following on Twitter through a fairly simple process: when I think of a creative piece of advice, I sometimes post it on my Twitter. Today, I have a few thousand followers. I'm no Gary Vaynerchuk. But I do have a few thousand followers, and sometimes that's all you need. I can now pretty easily interact with venture capitalists over Twitter and even befriend them, merely due to the fact that I focused on building a personal brand early on.

You can also access venture capitalists by knowing other people who know them in turn. This right here is a big reason why I like hanging around people who are older than me. They have connections that I do not have. I help them with what I know, like ranking websites in Google, and they offer me favors when I need them. I have literally been told "if you ever need money, just let me know," by some of my older connections. But believe it or not, these types of connections are not hard to find! In my opinion, it's fair to say that anyone who works in Silicon Valley or NYC at an above-average office job would be able to put you in touch with investors. You just have to start networking.

To hear pitches, we have partners across Canada so we tend to split things up geographically. For example, yesterday I went to Waterloo and I heard 6 pitches while I was there and that was me sitting in a room and another person would come in for half an hour and we'd just chat about the idea. That very first meeting they'll take me through a deck or I'll just ask questions. It's just getting a sense about whether the guy's an idiot. You know when you talk about the founder it's very hard for me to decide if a founder is great, in fact it's impossible but I can tell if he's a bozo and that's really my objective as a VC, to filter that guy out. And then see if the rest of the pitch looks reasonable. We do a lot over video conference. Probably 50%. People just drop by our office. Almost everything is by referral. If I get an unreferred email in my inbox, I'll just delete it.

SANJAY SINGHAL

CANADIAN VENTURE PARTNER, 500 STARTUPS

We started a friends and family round at $50k CAD. Then we had 3 rounds of angel with people we knew, which was a total of $180k. We did a series A too, but we raised $950k total.

For the series A, there were people from all over. It wasn't easy, Rick and Jason went down to the Valley to pitch. It's one of those things that domino effect. When somebody well known jumps on board, a lot of people jump on board. That's a really smart strategy because if you can get someone with a name then others will tag along.

OLI GARDNER

CO-FOUNDER, UNBOUNCE

This guy, Will Bunker, was on a trip out to Boston, he was speaking at an event here and he's based in Silicon Valley, he's one of the guys that started Match.com and he wanted to meet startups that are in town. The woman who was running the event reached out to me, asked if we were raising capital. I said we are, but not for the company that you think we are [but rather a spin off called Brass Monkey]. She sent off a deck about Red5 to Will. Will used Red5 in a previous company so he knew the open source project and I met with him when he was out here and subsequently met with him back out in Silicon Valley again and he was putting together a new fund and a new company called Growth Action. They were the first ones to come in on this round. And they introduced us to some other people, one of their LPs and you know closed out the round with their help.

CHRIS ALLEN

CO-FOUNDER, RED5

CLOSING THOUGHTS & CHECKLIST

• • • • • • •

I hope my advice and experience has served as an adequate beginner blueprint for you to become a Non-Technical Founder. My only objective when writing this book was to help you succeed. Thank you for taking your valuable time to read what I have to say.

To wrap things up, I will give you a broad checklist to follow. If you have more questions, go back to the relevant chapter, dig deeper into the concepts through other resources, or feel free to reach out to me directly through the contact form on my website. I'm always looking to make new connections.

If you are a beginner and you wish to have personalized help as you go along, feel free to ask about my consulting when you contact me. Lastly, if you enjoyed the book and want to do me a big favor, feel free to leave an honest review on Amazon with your feedback. Every single one helps.

Without further ado, here's your "big picture" checklist.

1. Think of an idea.
2. Validate your idea.
3. Create an MVP.
4. Validate your MVP.

5. Hire a developer.
6. Beta test your software.
7. Build out accompanying business assets.
8. Market your software.
9. Get customers; see success!

CLOSING THOUGHTS FROM MY CONTRIBUTORS

● ● ● ● ● ● ● ●

I think we covered a lot. You can talk about this stuff for days. There's so much that's possible in this space in terms of directions you can go and solutions. I'm a big proponent of when you have a product not starting from scratch. And what I mean by that is have some avenue to get your first users in the door. Have something, know somebody, talk to somebody, a blogger, an influencer, a chamber of commerce. Somewhere somehow there's somebody who has your audience and has their captive attention. You need to not be starting at zero. If you're a digital marketer and you built a tool for marketers, you probably know a few people who you could start off with and that's where a lot of products go bad is that they knew nobody and nothing and they bring an app to us and say we have zero users, what do we do. And that's a problem.

ILAN NASS

FOUNDER, TAKTICAL DIGITAL

———————

One trap a lot of non-technical people fall into is that they think the idea is the business. So it's like, well, I can't let anybody else have my idea cause

179

they'll go off and code it and they're the ones who are gonna make billions of dollars and I'm left out in the cold. It's just not how it works. You have to get out there and tell your idea and your vision to as many people as you can, start to get people on board and you know 99 out of 100 potential technical cofounders will not steal your idea and the 100th one—karma's gonna get him, eventually. You're way better off propagating the idea, demonstrating your excitement, getting somebody else coming up and saying that's really cool, can I work with you on that or I'd' love to get involved somehow. Get out there, be enthusiastic and talk about your idea to as many people as you possibly can. And you will find your technical cofounder.

SANJAY SINGHAL

CANADIAN VENTURE PARTNER, 500 STARTUPS

You need to build a team. You can't build a technology team by itself. You've got to have the other flipped side of the equation. You've got to have a marketing and sales person combined with technology to find the difference and to explore the differences. You've also got to try to develop disruptive technology. You've got to have a persistence and tenacity because those things are all key hallmarks of building and having the staying power as an entrepreneur. That's why so many things fail. And finally, I think the last thing I'd recommend is that people get schooled up on what's called RFI—reach, frequency, and impact. These are just core stones as you're laying the foundation to any successful company. You've gotta have the right reach, you've gotta have the right frequency, and you've got to have something impactful so people remember who you are and what you can deliver to them. I think these are some of the things I've lived by and being successful in my career in several countries, and you know getting the kind of accomplishments taking something from a kernel of an idea to be able to run with it. I think everybody has an idea, where it stops with most people is the capability of taking an idea and turning it into a commercial enterprise. And that's where the rubber meets the road, so to speak and that's where some of those other areas you've just gotta have them, otherwise you're just gambling so much with your time and energy.

JEFF MAYNARD

PRESIDENT AND CEO, BIOMETRIC SIGNATURE ID

You know like when I started the company, I had $1100 in the bank, I was about to get evicted from my apartment in New York. I had come from a big fancy job in Hollywood, moved to New York and that company went under. I was left on my own and couldn't get a job. You succeed because you have to succeed. You have no other option. At this point in my life when I'm done with 87AM (whatever contracts or sales I have with it), will I go into something else and, of course, go about it a very different way and get other people's money to invest and scale it a different way? Absolutely. But at that point in my life, to begin, the only way that I could have been successful was the fact that I had no other option but to be successful. I could have taken a job for $50,000 somewhere and that would be my job and I would be working myself up the ranks but the fact that I couldn't get the job it pushed me into a position where I had to create something and it just so happened it turned into a quarter of a billion dollar company.

ADAM CUNNINGHAM

FOUNDER, 87AM

Carol Roth is the only female contributor who offered her time to me for an interview, so I asked her if she had any advice for women entrepreneurs in particular.

Yes, stop thinking of yourself as a woman entrepreneur or a black entrepreneur, etc. You are an entrepreneur, period. Your chromosomes, skin color, and other factors outside of your control have zero effect on your ability to be successful. Network with people who are already successful and think big. Don't let anyone tell you differently or make you feel less. You are an entrepreneur. End of story.

CAROL ROTH

TV CONTRIBUTOR AND BEST-SELLING AUTHOR

I would say before you build anything, try to do everything you can to understand whether it's a good idea or not. Even through Upwork, building an app for a website can cost a significant amount of money and the odds are that your idea is not that good, at least, the first version of it is not that good. By talking to potential customers, by getting their input you'll make iterations on it and it's much cheaper to iterate on the idea on paper and on Post-it notes than it is to do it with the code. You'll do it faster and you'll do it cheaper so try to before you go hire a designer then hire engineers. Start with a pen and a piece of paper and talk to your audience and iterate until you tell yourself that it's really going to work and then you know start executing on it and building the software and building the code strategy around it and building the rest of the company.

STEPHANE KASRIEL

CEO, UPWORK

The Internet is still full of opportunities and continues developing daily. The new directions and business spheres are emerging: neural networks, the Internet of Things (IoT), blockchain. Everyone can make a mark on the world wide web today, just like 20 years ago.

SASHA ANDRIEIEV

CEO, JELVIX

So at Hotjar we're big fans of just writing about our story and what we've learned as opposed to being prescriptive and telling people what to do or not to do. I think the most valuable thing is to share what we've gone through and hopefully that can impact others. The whole passion fallacy idea is based on the fact that most of us tend to kind of think of ideas for businesses based on what we know and what we love and what is directly visible to us, right. But I think the big turning point for me, and this took quite long so maybe I'm a little bit slow but as long as I get there I'm happy with that. I think the big turning point for me is that I worked in marketing for so long but I didn't really realize what marketing was about for so long. Marketing is not about getting the word out about your user or attracting them to the site or getting a signup. Marketing is all about what we talked about before, niche or what is this, how big is this collection of people that we can approach and how many customers can we deliver value to. Stop thinking about how do I make $1,000,000 and instead think about how do I deliver value to 1,000,000 customers, and when you start thinking like that you start looking at whether there's really a market here or not. And that's why internally I've started to write marketing with a dash between "market" and "ing." It's this emphasis on if you want to start a business, make sure you understand that there is a market that exists. They are aware of the problem and they have what I like to call a budget allocated to it. So, it doesn't need to be necessarily an actual budget in their accounting department, but my point is they've already, in their mind, allocated money to it. Let me give you an example before Hotjar. We created a tool for restaurants, retail outlets, hotels and whatnot to use, to basically grow their business. It was based on our knowledge of growing businesses and this tool was fantastic and it was guaranteed to have results. The problem was the people we were trying to speak to did not have a budget allocated to this tool. In their mind, spending money on this was not part of the plan and when you want to persuade people to do that, you're kind of changing their behavior and that is incredibly difficult to do. So that is rule 1. Market size, is there a market and do they have a budget because in the end the market is not just the account of the people but what is the total budget available. #2 is *addressability. Like how easy is it for you to find people in this market and can they be approached? Going back to the example of the restaurant's thing. The first thing we were hit by was that these guys don't have a proper office and usually working at night, and we were working in the morning. So, we were hit by that addressability issue. And the fact that we were based in Malta and we had more of a worldwide approach and we started to realize this was going to be a huge operational challenge. And, number 3, what is your unfair advantage? We live at the time when technology is free and the idea you have many more people you need to have some kind of advantage. And this is where passion can be helpful. If you've spent a lot of time or you understand the market or maybe you're really well-connected to the typical user in the market. So, I'd say these three things are much more important than just being passionate about something. It's not enough to be passionate about cars to think that you can build a car business. It's not enough to be passionate about software to just build a software company. You need those three ingredients. Identifying and sizing up that market and making sure they are addressable and having some kind of unfair advantage. That would be the loaded advice I would leave everyone with.*

DR. DAVID DARMANIN

CO-FOUNDER, HOTJAR

If you only have an idea, you're at step 1 of a million steps. So it's really worthless. The only thing you can do is figure out what the next step is. It's different in any case so there's not one step that I can give but typically if you're moving forward, you'll figure it out along the way. With a new idea, I would say the best thing to do is be able to validate the idea in some kind of cost-effective way that doesn't take a long of time to do, and allows you to be flexible and change things because as soon as you stick to an idea that nobody wants then you'll be wasting time and money. More than anything, how can you create something that some people will pay for as fast as possible, that's really your goal.

WYATT JOZWOWSKI
CO-FOUNDER, DEMIO

It's my opinion that I think we've barely scratched the surface of what technology can do for mankind. The ability that we have to niche, you know, like you could find 100,000 people to pay you money monthly, it's insane! Like that used to be considered like oh, it's not mass enough, like no! So, I think what's going happen, in my opinion, is we're headed to where development and design are going to become commoditized and creativity is going to be the only thing that entrepreneurs do and so it's literally going to be only a bunch of weekend events and new ideas and combine them. You can imagine like even now with Squarespace like you don't need, I mean to launch something you don't need anyone, you can just do it yourself. I think that's happening soon for development, where literally we're just moving Lego pieces around then suddenly, I mean if you can build something that's making you a $100 grand a month and it's just you, you're a rich man.

BLAKE SMITH
CO-FOUNDER, CLADWELL

I am forever in debt to my mentors for everything they have taught me over the past eight years. I have tried to repay them in the past, but each one has refused everything I have proposed. Instead, they requested that I pay it forward and mentor others when the time comes. Now that this book is finally complete, I am hopeful I will be able to do so on a larger scale. I've sat with others on Skype before, but one-on-one has its limitations. I hope this book will help you succeed in a serious way, even if we never get the chance to meet.

JOSH MACDONALD

FEATURED INTERVIEWEES

• • • • • • • •

Chris Allen is an international speaker, software inventor and entrepreneur. He co-founded the open source Flash server Red5, where he and his team of volunteers reverse engineered Flash's RTMP protocol.

Sasha Andrieiev is the founder, owner and CEO of Jelvix. Jelvix is one of the leading software development companies on Upwork with over $1 million in paid jobs, a job completion rate of 100% and a steady flow of 5.0 star reviews.

James Blackwell is a co-founder of BuzzSumo, a search engine that lets you analyze trending content and influencers across social networks. Thousands of agencies, brands and publishers use BuzzSumo Pro.

Adam Cunningham is the CEO and founder of 87 AM. 87AM is the world's leading full-service digital agency focusing on arts, entertainment, and culture with clients such as 20th Century Fox, Lionsgate, IMAX, Paramount Pictures, and Universal.

Dr David Darmanin is an entrepreneur and conversion optimization consultant. He is the founder and CEO of Hotjar, an intuitive research and optimization tool used by companies of all sizes. Some of their clients include Nintendo, Microsoft, intuit, Columbia, and VistaPrint.

187

John Doherty is the founder of Credo, a company that helps businesses find the right consultant to grow their business. Previously, John served as the Senior Manager of Growth Marketing at Trulia Rentals.

Ben Donkor is the social media analyst at Microsoft UK, where he provides social media insights and recommendations for key stakeholder groups across the company. Outside of Microsoft, he freelances for clients like Adobe, BrandWatch, and Social Media Week.

Adam Draper is the founder and managing director of Boost VC, which has invested in over 180 startups, spanning over 30 countries, since 2012. Before starting his incubator, Adam co-founded Xpert Financial while in his senior year at UCLA.

Oli Gardner is a co-founder of Unbounce, a landing page creation software used by companies like New Balance, The New York Times, and Vimeo. He was the first marketer at Unbounce, leading the company to over 14,000 customers.

Daniel Gross is a partner at YCombinator, a seed accelerator that invested in companies like Stripe, Teespring, AirBnB and Weebly. Before joining YCombinator, he co-founded the personal assistant app Cue, and was acquired by Apple in 2013, where he continued to work until 2017.

Peter Hudson is the founder and CEO of Shelfie, an app where users take a picture of their bookshelf (a "shelfie") and the app will auto-tag all the books on your shelf and then let them download digital copies of their paper library. Shelfie was acquired by Kobo in 2017.

Wyatt Jozwowski is a co-founder of Demio, a webinar platform that focuses on reliability and simplicity. Before Demio, he sold a number of different software. At just 21 years old, he is the youngest person interviewed.

Stephane Kasriel is the CEO of Upwork, the world's largest freelancing website. Before joining Upwork (then oDesk), he served as an executive for companies like PayPal and Zong. He was appointed to be the CEO of Upwork, directing the company through the merger of oDesk and Elance.

Josh Luber is the CEO and co-founder of StockX, a marketplace for rare, genuine sneakers. They mediate the transaction, making sure no one gets scammed. Leveraging his knowledge on sneakers, he gave a TED Talk, which now has over 1.8 million views.

David Markovich is a NYC-based consultant and the founder of Online Geniuses, a vetted internet marketing community with meetups at over 15 locations worldwide. He is the organizer of NY Internet Marketing, a meetup with over 2500 members and is well-networked in the marketing community.

Jeff Maynard is the founder of Biometric Signature ID, an identity verification software. His company works with some of the largest institutions in higher education, financial services, online gaming, and healthcare to ensure critical information stays secure.

Ilan Nass is the founder of Taktical Digital, a leading NYC marketing firm and one of my advisors. Taktical has helped grow world-class startups such as WeWork, Homepolish, Splash, Artsy, and Fueled. He has a wide variety of experience building and growing companies.

Brad Owen is a co-founder of NeverBounce, a real-time email cleaning service trusted by over 35,000 organizations, including a solid portion of the Fortune 500s. Before NeverBounce, he ran a marketing agency that he also founded.

Carol Roth is a business advisor, investor, entrepreneur, and best-selling author of The Entrepreneur Equation. She also "plays herself on TV," as a reality TV show judge, media contributor, and host of Microsoft's Office Small Business Academy.

Dan Sharp is a co-founder of Screaming Frog, a search engine marketing agency also known for creating a powerful SEO tool for crawling the web, used by hundreds of thousands of people worldwide. Dan has been working as a marketer since 2005, making him one of the most experienced players in the game.

Sanjay Singhal is the Canadian Venture Partner for 500 Startups and founder of Audiobooks.com. He also has invested in over 20 startups.

Blake Smith is the co-founder of Cladwell, an app that helps you create more outfit combinations, with fewer clothing items. Cladwell is a member of the 17th batch of startups in 500 Startups' accelerator program.

Richard Stumpf is the founder of Atlas Music Group, a full service music publishing company with clients such as Counting Crows, Van Halen, and many others. He brings a unique skillset from the business world, outside of the tech space.

Frank van Mierlo is the founder of 1366 Technologies, a manufacturing company that makes the world's most cost effective silicon wafers. Before 1366, he founded Bluefin Robotics, a company that creates autonomous underwater vehicles which was sold in 2005 to Battelle.

Scott Ward is the social media coordinator of Denver Broncos. Before the Broncos, he was in charge of media relations at the Colorado Avalanche. With his primary focus being social media, he brings a specialized skillset to the book.

ACKNOWLEDGEMENTS

● ● ● ● ● ● ●

In no particular order, I'd like to thank anyone who had interest in my success or helped me over the years. Friends, family, teachers, and everyone else, you know who you are.

I'd like to thank Don for seeing so much in me before I made a dime, Ilan for teaching me so much about sales, Bruce for the endless advice on everything in and outside of business, Joseph for letting me bounce endless ideas off you, Greg for pushing me into the deep end to pursue what became a great success, Joshua for the invaluable affiliate advice, and the dozens of others in my industry who always lent advice to a young mind. Thank you to all of my other mentors who have come and gone over the years as well.

Once again, thank you to the amazing contributors who took time out of their busy lives to offer their wisdom to my readers.

Thank you to my amazing customers. Whether by email and phone, I've talked with many of you over the years. Without you, I would have no business success and most certainly would not be here writing a book on building and selling software. I would be nothing without you.

Thank you to my parents for putting up with all the crazy ventures I attempt, and all their pieces of advice on all things adult.

Lastly, I'd like to thank the man this book was dedicated to, my late grandfather, John Johnson, who was always impressed with everything I did, big or small.

Morgan James
Speakers Group

We connect Morgan James published authors with live and online events and audiences who will benefit from their expertise.

Morgan James makes all of our titles available
through the Library for All Charity Organization.

www.LibraryForAll.org